THE PHILOSOPHY OF RELIGION

The
Philosophy of Religion

Thomas McPherson

Senior Lecturer in Philosophy
University College of South Wales and Monmouthshire

D. VAN NOSTRAND COMPANY LTD
LONDON

TORONTO NEW YORK
PRINCETON, NEW JERSEY

D. VAN NOSTRAND COMPANY LTD.
358 Kensington High Street, London, W.14

D. VAN NOSTRAND COMPANY INC.
120 Alexander Street, Princeton, New Jersey
24 West 40th Street, New York 18

D. VAN NOSTRAND COMPANY (CANADA) LTD.
25 Hollinger Road, Toronto 16

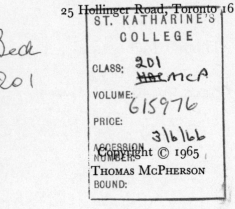
Library of Congress Catalog Card No. 65–20160

PRINTED IN GREAT BRITAIN BY
J. W. ARROWSMITH, BRISTOL, ENGLAND

To DILYS
ALSO SIÂN, DYLAN
AND CATRIN

Preface

OVER the past twenty years or so, the philosophy of religion has become a major interest of professional philosophers in the English-speaking world. The present book is intended to provide for students and others a general introduction to the subject—a background against which current discussion can be seen in perspective. The book is fairly traditional in plan. The themes that are treated are those that teachers of the philosophy of religion have generally thought it necessary to consider. Some things—particularly perhaps the interpretation of Anselm—are not in all respects orthodox. Still, philosophy thrives on disagreement.

The philosophy of religion is both a branch of philosophy and a branch of theology. This can lead to the writing of books ostensibly on the same subject which nevertheless are markedly different from each other in tone; or, which is worse, that aim to be all things to all men and attempt an unfortunate amalgamation of the philosophical and the homiletic. In the present book the subject is treated strictly as a branch of philosophy. This has not prevented me from stressing when appropriate the part played in religion by faith and commitment.

Chapter 12 has already appeared in print, in the *Proceedings of the Aristotelian Society*, *1959–60* (New Series, Vol. LX); and elsewhere in the book I have made use of some sentences and paragraphs from articles published in *Mind*, July 1957 (New Series, Vol. LXVI), *Philosophy*, July 1957 (Vol. XXXII), and *The Church Quarterly Review*, April–June 1960 (Vol. CLXI). I am grateful to the editors for their willingness to allow me to use this material again. I am glad also to have the opportunity of expressing my gratitude to the following, who did me the kindness of reading parts of the book in draft, and who made many helpful suggestions: Mr. D. R. Ap-Thomas, Mr. Michael Durrant, Professor J. L. Evans, Professor Ronald W. Hepburn, Professor H. D. Lewis, Miss Gwynneth Matthews, Professor C. W. K. Mundle, and Professor Ninian Smart. What remains in the way of error and infelicity is, of course, entirely my own responsibility. I wish also to thank Avis Green for her efficient typing of the manuscript. My wife and children have had to endure my preoccupation with this book for altogether too long, and have had less of my company than they ought. My wife, in particular, might understandably have refused to have anything further to do with it. She has, in fact, made time to check the typescript and read the proofs. I thank her for this, and for her patience during the months of composition.

T. McP.

Cardiff
September 1964

Contents

CHAPTER 1

What is the Philosophy of Religion?

PHILOSOPHY is a remote and abstract subject. Such at any rate is the popular opinion. It is certainly the case that much of the time of philosophers is taken up with inquiries that have little obvious bearing upon the practical affairs of human life. Nevertheless, there are certain branches of philosophy of which this has always been less true than of others. The study of ethics may not make someone a morally better man: the study of political philosophy may not make him a more obedient subject: the study of the philosophy of religion may not make him a Christian or an atheist. These results, however, *may* follow. And in the past some philosophers wrote on these subjects with the express intention that practical results of this kind should indeed follow. In particular, this has not infrequently been the aim of writers on the philosophy of religion.

It is not the aim of the present book. Philosophy is nobody's handmaiden. At the same time, the concepts and arguments of religion are such that practical results are likely still to follow on philosophical inquiry into them, however abstract the philosopher's methods may seem. What I am attempting in this book is some clarification of certain concepts and arguments. The explicit drawing of conclusions is very much secondary to this. But the reader is free to draw his own conclusions. The inquiry is far from 'remote and abstract', if this means that there is nothing in the activity of the philosopher that ought to have any effect *at all* upon what people believe and how they act.

The book is an introduction to the philosophy of religion, built around what I take to be the central theme of the subject: the place of reason in religion. A typically philosophical examination of religion—which is to say, a rational, clarificatory examination —is bound to consider before anything else the question whether religion itself is to be described as rational or as non-rational. From that centre all more particular questions can be seen as radiating.

Certainly, this question can have no simple answer of the form 'Religion is rational' or 'Religion is non-rational'. These expressions do not have a single, agreed use. So much is this so that a man who says 'Religion is non-rational' (meaning one thing) may actually have less in common with another who utters the same words (but meaning something else) than he has with a third who says 'Religion is rational'. I hope in the succeeding chapters to bring out some of the complexity of the use of 'rational' and 'non-rational' in connexion with religion.

The discussion in this book is for the most part limited to the Christian religion. It is not that I think it impossible to provide what might be called a philosophy of religion in general, as opposed to the philosophy of a particular religion or group of religions. There are, however, difficulties attached to such an enterprise, and it is a matter of some importance to note these.

To begin with, anything that sets out to be a study of religion in general is bound to be inconclusive. For it is attempting to isolate the highest common factor of religion—that which all religions have in common. But if there is such a thing, it is, in the nature of the case, bound to be of a highly general, non-specific character. The respects in which religions may be identical are almost certain to be few in number, and vague. It is the respects in which they differ that are likely to be numerous and to lend themselves to clear statement and profitable discussion at length.

Any account of religion, if it is to be adequate, must recognize a number of elements in it—emotional, belief, moral, ritual, and possibly institutional. Terminology used in listing these varies. Sometimes it is said that the elements reduce to three, and on this assumption a usefully alliterative formula is: creed, code, and cult. Clearly, it is only possible to discuss these general concepts profitably if they are 'cashed' in terms of some one or more of the world's recognized religions. It is the particular forms taken by creeds, codes, and cults that are interesting and important, not just the fact that a religion has these three elements; and to have recognized this is to have passed beyond an interest in religion in general to one in religions in particular.

In the second place, anyone who sets out on the study of religion in general exposes himself to the temptation of presenting too narrow a view. Even the threefold characterization just noted is likely not to seem general enough. It will seem natural to press on beyond this stage to one of even greater generality: a stage where, most commonly, the 'real essence' of religion is found to lie in a special type of *experience*—perhaps emotional, perhaps partly emotional and partly cognitive. If indeed there is such a thing as the highest common factor of all religions, this is probably it. But to isolate this from the other things that go to make up the actual religions of the world would be to convey a misleading impression. I do not deny the central importance in a religion like Christianity of such experiences—and this theme will be discussed in a later chapter—but if Christianity is represented in such terms as these too exclusively it is not represented fairly. An account of religion that does not adequately describe Christianity, *ipso facto* does not adequately describe religion.

Further, philosophy is largely concerned with language; for it is sentences and arguments that are the natural material for a clarificatory activity. Hence the philosopher will find more to say about the belief element in religion—the most highly verbalized element—than about the others. This means, once more, that if he is to discuss religion from his own point of view at all usefully, he will be concentrating his attention on the respects in which religions are different, and not on those in which they are the same; for it is in the details of their beliefs that religions differ most, as it is in their moral, and especially their emotional, aspects that they differ least. It follows, incidentally, that the philosopher will find particular possibilities for his own kind of activity if he studies a religion like Christianity, in which the element of verbalization—in the Bible, in theological controversy, and in hymns and countless sermons—is extremely strong.

So, then, the search for the highest common factor of all religions will offer the philosopher little scope. At the same time, he will himself be at fault if he gives the impression that the belief element is more than just what particularly interests him as a philosopher—if in concentrating upon it he gives the impression that it is itself the real essence of all religion.

If what I have so far argued is agreed, the next step is a simple one. The philosopher, seeing that he must concentrate his attention on a specific religion or group of religions in which the belief element is strongly developed, will naturally turn to the religion that he knows best. Almost certainly, this means in our society that he will turn to Christianity.

This is how it comes about that the philosophy of religion means in practice the philosophy of the Christian religion. Certainly this is what it means for the present book.

Still, what I have said is not intended to suggest that the study of one religion has nothing to gain from the study of others. The philosopher, in considering the Christian concept of creation, or providence, or incarnation, may indeed find it useful to compare such concepts with similar ones in other religions. (See, for instance, Smart (1) and (2), *passim*.) But it is not an essential part of his job to do this. The philosophy of religion needs to be distinguished from the comparative study of religion (or history of religions, a near-synonym). The latter is largely a positive study, which aims to describe the various forms that religion has taken in the world and to speculate about its origins. By contrast, the philosophy of religion is a critical study. The philosopher of the Christian religion does not describe the Christian religion. He concerns himself principally with attempting to clarify the problems of meaning that arise in connexion with its belief element. The philosopher of religion may learn much from the comparative student of religion, and *vice versa*; but the two subjects differ in aim. Some writers claiming the name of philosophers of religion occupy themselves largely with describing in detail, and with critical faculties suspended, the features of religion. Such writers are engaged in the phenomenology of religion; but in my view this can only be a preliminary to the philosophy of religion proper. The interesting part of philosophy—and the peculiarly philosophical part—is the activity of getting things clear. I do not wish to deny, of course, that the comparative study of religions may itself throw up problems calling for a philosophical treatment.

CHAPTER 2

The Contemporary View

In the pursuit of our central inquiry—into the place of reason in religion—we may take as our starting point the contemporary climate of opinion about religion. There is, I think, a strong tendency at the present time to describe religion as non-rational or irrational (which of these terms is chosen commonly depends on whether the speaker approves of religion or disapproves of it); and it is by noting some of the predisposing causes lying behind this tendency that we can best begin.

This distinctively contemporary view of religion did not, of course, come into being Melchizedek-like, without father or mother, in the middle of the twentieth century. Its roots lie further back, and its development can easily be traced. For our present purposes we may take Immanuel Kant (1724–1804) as marking the beginning of the process that culminates in the contemporary view, though if our interests were primarily historical we could go back a good deal earlier. Before Kant, religion was generally regarded as rational, in the sense that some religious beliefs were thought capable of conclusive demonstration, and all, or nearly all, capable of being expressed in meaningful assertions. Kant, by his destructive criticism of the theistic arguments and his wholehearted insistence that we must sweep away knowledge in the sphere of religion in favour of faith, set a fashion which, though not entirely new, was enormously influential. Kant stands on the dividing line between the usual traditional view of religion and the usual modern view. What Kant began Søren Kierkegaard (1813–55) consolidated. Throughout the nineteenth century the process continued. Christians began to develop an interest in the

6

other great world religions and in primitive religion, and began to ask questions about the nature and origins of religion in general—questions which, as I pointed out in the previous chapter, are in the nature of the case linked with its non-rational aspects. Hegel (1770–1831) regarded religion as picture thinking, to be superseded by philosophy—that is, by his, Hegel's, philosophy, a philosophy that was itself a kind of sublimation of religion. Schleiermacher (1768–1834) gave impetus to an interest in 'religious experience' and in the 'emotional' side of religion, and thus in yet another way helped to bring about the tendency to reject the 'rational' character of Christianity. And there was the influence of nineteenth-century atheistic rationalism; and that of Darwinism.

It would be wrong, however, to give the impression of a century and a half of happy co-operation. Although from our present-day point of view the individuals and schools of thought I have referred to may appear as fellow-labourers towards a single end, this was not always how they appeared to each other. The differences between them were real enough, and in concentrating, as I do here, on a very general kind of likeness, I am far from wishing to deny this. But the onlooker sees most of the game; and when we look back upon these movements we can see that there was more similarity of view than the nineteenth-century thinkers themselves would have been glad to acknowledge.

There are, equally, likenesses among more recent views that sometimes escape their holders. To take a sample from the large class of twentieth-century thinkers whose pronouncements on religion have been widely read: Karl Barth; Aldous Huxley, in his curiously named, or perhaps one should say, curiously meant, *The Perennial Philosophy*, and in his writings on mescalin experiences (Huxley (2) and (3)); Freud and his followers; Jung and his; Logical Positivists; some Existentialists; Scientific Humanists; —all these are united in regarding religion as in some sense 'not an affair of the reason'; though in how precisely they understand this, and in what they would put forward as the true view of religion, they present no such united front.

A belief in its non-rationality is, then, the distinctively contemporary view of religion. But I am aware that not absolutely everybody at the present time shares it. I am aware, too, that there are thinkers who try to combine traditional and contemporary; that is, that there are mild as well as extreme forms of the contemporary view. Perhaps I need hardly say, either, that in calling this view 'contemporary' I do not mean to prejudge the issue by implying either approval or disapproval of it. It is neither meritorious nor the opposite to be in the swim where ideas and beliefs are concerned. Ultimately, it must be on other grounds than that of fashion that we choose between them. On the other hand, the fact of their being fashionable can sufficiently justify one in examining them at length.

It will be advisable now to look more closely at one or two of the more important among the influences that have gone to create the contemporary view. I shall not in the present chapter be raising questions about whether these, or other, influences provide good grounds for the contemporary view. The assessing of reasons and arguments will come later. At the moment, I am concerned only with the fact that men have come to think of religion as non-rational. I am not yet concerned with what precisely they mean by this; nor with whether they are justified in thinking of religion thus.

The first thing that we need to consider here is the influence of science and scientific ways of thought. The contemporary climate of opinion in general is to a large extent the creation of scientific attitudes. There has long been the semblance, and sometimes the reality, of conflict between science and traditional religion; and the contemporary view of religion serves as a reminder of the extent to which that conflict has been won by science. The last hundred years or so, beginning with the controversy over evolution that followed on the publication of Darwin's *Origin of Species* in 1859, have witnessed a progressive retreat on the part of religious believers. The success of science in many fields led, as it had done in the seventeenth century, to a conviction that the way to success in any field lies in the adoption of scientific methods. From this point of view, religion is seen either as an obstacle (in that its attitudes are held to be totally opposed to those of science) or as a game but inefficient competitor (in that to some extent religion and science are held to be doing the same job, but science to be doing it better). These are, of course, two quite different attitudes to religion: on the one hand, that it is totally unscientific; on the other, that it is merely insufficiently scientific. These attitudes may perhaps be made clearer if we consider one or two of the forms that they have taken in recent years.

Logical Positivism is the name given to the philosophy taught by the Vienna Circle, a group of thinkers that flourished under the leadership of Moritz Schlick, and whose influence was considerable in the English-speaking philosophical world in the 'thirties and 'forties. (Further information may be found in, e.g. Ayer (2).) The driving force behind the Vienna Circle was science. Although its members were themselves not all scientists, what they had in common was an interest in science and a desire to apply scientific methods in philosophy. The central tenet of Logical Positivism is its doctrine of meaning—the Verification Principle—according to which a proposition is meaningful only if either (1) it is analytic (i.e. its truth is guaranteed by its form; e.g. propositions in mathematics, or propositions like 'If it is raining then it is raining'), or (2) it is empirically verifiable (i.e. there is some agreed procedure, involving observation or experiment, of establishing its truth or falsehood). This is really an attempt to convert the central features of scientific method (the use by scientists of mathematics and of observation and experiment) into criteria of meaning which are claimed to have universal validity. What is relevant to our present purpose is that Logical Positivists held as a consequence of the Verification Principle that religious and theological propositions are meaningless. They are not analytic; neither are they empirically verifiable: they must accordingly be senseless. (See Ayer (1), Chap. VI—also Ayer and Copleston.) To say this is to say that religion is irrational —irrational in that religious belief is incapable of expression in a set of meaningful assertions: what the religious believer utters must be literally nonsense. Here, then, is a view according to which religion, because meaningless, is totally opposed to science, which is not only meaningful but actually sets the standard for meaningfulness.

Sigmund Freud (1856–1939), in the course of his many discussions of religion, makes explicit comparisons between it and
science; and Freud would claim to be himself writing as a
scientist. Religion means turning one's back upon reality; science
means coming to grips with reality. Religion deals in fantasies;
science in facts. Indeed, the future of civilization ultimately
depends upon the replacing of the irrational attitude of religion
by the rational attitude of science. Freud relates how his son, on
being told a fairy story, would inquire whether it was true; and
on being told that it was not, would scornfully refuse to take any
further interest in it (Freud (4), p. 51). Religion is on the level of
fairy stories; the literal-minded son is a symbolic scientist. Freud,
we need to note, does not dismiss the utterances of religious
believers as meaningless. They may well have a meaning; but
the reason why they are not worth taking seriously is because they
have no bearing upon the really important questions, i.e. scientific
questions, about the nature of the world in which we live and
about human nature; and they have no bearing upon these
questions because they are merely the products of wish-fulfilment.

Freud's view of religion is a kind of half-way house between
Logical Positivism and the view that we are now to consider. It
is not uncommonly argued at the present day that religion is
outmoded because the job it once performed has now been taken
over by science, which is doing it very much better. This is the
view of religion as a kind of unsophisticated science, which sets
out to make sense of our experience by providing an account of
man, of the universe, and of man's place in the universe. Religion
has, admittedly, aimed at doing something like this; and there
can be no doubt that science is far better at providing at least
some kind of explanation of our ordinary experience. This view
of religion sees it as working the same soil as science, but, because
it is using antique implements, working it with much less efficiency
and precision. Religion ought, then, to be pensioned off; not
because it is meaningless, as the Logical Positivists claimed; not
even, as Freud claimed, because its influence is pernicious in that
it belongs to the world of fantasy and blinds its adherents to
reality; but because, although it does a perfectly proper, and,
indeed, a vitally important, job, it just does not do it well enough.

This view, like those of the Logical Positivists and Freud, implies the irrationality of religion—but this time in the sense that a rational man is bound to reject an inefficient way of getting a job done in favour of an efficient way.

In some quarters it has been fashionable to draw an analogy between religion and art. This needs to be worked out somewhat differently according to whether the analogy suggested is between the creative artist and the creative religious thinker or saint, or between the ordinary person who appreciates works of art and the ordinary religious believer. I shall be considering only the first of these. In some of what follows I shall for convenience be constructing positions which I do not necessarily claim are held by nameable thinkers in precisely the form in which I present them.

If in the interests of simplification we leave literature out of account, initially the artist may with some plausibility be said to work on a non-rational level. It would be generally agreed that the different art forms cannot be translated into each other without loss. You cannot turn a piece of music into a painting, or a painting into a dance. What you can do is create another work of art in the other medium which aims to convey in its own way what was conveyed by the original; but it will still be a different work. In particular, you cannot re-express *in words* with total adequacy what a painter, a composer, a choreographer, has tried to do. This is all a very familiar story.

What is meant in the present context by saying that the artist works on a non-rational level is simply the point just made— that no one, with words, can re-create exactly what the artist is creating by non-verbal means: rationality, it is assumed for the purposes of the present argument, involves verbalization. Even the verbal artist can, if someone insists on this complication, be brought into the picture at this stage. It may well be the case that the literary use of words involves something over and above the non-literary use or uses of words: if the ordinary, unpoetical man tries to re-express a poem by using language in his ordinary, unpoetical way, he is bound to fail.

One way in which all this can be put is the following. The

artist is someone who has a special insight into the nature of
things, which he seeks to express in his works of art. He cannot
adequately convey this insight otherwise than by expressing it in
his art. The creative religious man, similarly, it is suggested, has
a special insight into the nature of things, which he expresses in
religious utterances (which are akin to poetry), in the teaching of
a religio-moral policy, in the founding and recommending of
particular ritual practices, etc. He, too, it would be claimed,
cannot say what his insight is, otherwise than in the terms of his
religion; and even the verbal utterances of his religion contain,
like the writings of the literary artist, more than meets the
unliterary or non-religious eye, and are not capable of translation
into matter of fact, literal language.

We are not bound, however, to express the situation in terms
of 'insight'. It is doubtful, indeed, whether a description of the
artist as someone 'with a special kind of insight into things' really
means very much. The point can be made equally well, if less
imaginatively, by saying simply that the artist is someone who
creates works of art (a truism) and that, as a matter of fact, the
works of art he creates cannot easily and adequately be explained
in language, or, if he is a literary artist, in language used in an
other than literary way. The distinction that I am assuming here
between literary and non-literary uses of language, is, admittedly,
not a very clear one, and I would not in fact want to press it very
far. There are certainly some literary artists—indeed, most
novelists and dramatists—who use language, for the most part,
in a way not markedly dissimilar from non-literary uses of language, if we assume that there are such uses. If literary artists were
ignored entirely in the present context the basic argument would
not be affected; and there is perhaps no justification, in any case,
for supposing that exactly the same account must always be given
of all the art forms.

Without entering into controversies—so often acrimonious—
about 'modern art', we can at least note the relevance to our
present subject of those twentieth-century movements or individuals in the arts that have attracted the label 'irrational': sur-
realism in painting, for instance, or, more recently, action
painting; atonalism in music; the themes, if not their treatment,

of much of Kafka's writing, and the treatment, if not the themes, of Joyce's *Finnegans Wake*. To call a thing 'irrational', as we have noted already, tends to imply, and to invite, condemnation of it, as to call it 'non-rational' generally does not; and the issue of rationality versus irrationality in art is usually raised in the first place by opponents rather than supporters of modern movements. Let me substitute the comparatively neutral 'non-rational' for the more tendentious 'irrational'. Now, it seems unexceptionable to apply the description 'non-rational' to things such as those I have just mentioned. Certainly, the question 'What does this *mean*?' arises more acutely in such cases than in those of more traditional kinds of art. Rationality is generally a matter of degree. Much art may be called non-rational; but some kinds of art may well be said to be more non-rational than others.

'As Gregor Samsa awoke one morning from uneasy dreams he found himself transformed in his bed into a gigantic insect. He was lying on his hard, as it were armour-plated, back and when he lifted his head a little he could see his dome-like brown belly divided into stiff arched segments on top of which the bed-quilt could hardly keep in position and was about to slide off completely. His numerous legs, which were pitifully thin compared to the rest of his bulk, waved helplessly before his eyes.' The rest of Franz Kafka's story of the unfortunate commercial traveller Gregor Samsa (*Metamorphosis*) is as simple and down to earth as this, its opening. On one level, no one can be in doubt about what is being said in the story. Yet, on another level, no one can be certain what is being said. This may be true of much good art; but not all good art chooses themes that fly in the face of what the plain, unimaginative man might class as reasonable or even as meaningful. (So much the worse for plainness and unimaginativeness!) The period during which, as I have said, the view of religion as non-rational has been developing—the past century and a half or so—is also the period that begins in art with the Romantic Revival, and this is no coincidence: these are different aspects of the same phenomenon. What must now strike us as the crudity and obviousness of the 'supernatural' themes of writers of about the end of the eighteenth and the beginning of the nineteenth centuries, even when those writers are as great as

Coleridge, has given way to the sophisticated matter-of-factness of a Kafka; but Kafka and Coleridge, even so, form part of the same 'non-rational' trend. And it seems to me that the contemporary climate of opinion about art has helped to dispose people towards the non-rational view of religion.

It may be well if I repeat two points made earlier. First, 'rational' and 'non-rational' are terms with many meanings. I have not attempted to be consistent in my use of them. Indeed, the more variety in their use, the more they shift and change meaning between one sentence and the next, the better. We shall have all the more material to work on when we come to impose some order on them. Secondly, and following from the previous point, one man's non-rationality is another man's rationality. It does not matter particularly, for instance, whether Kafka's writings are described as rational or as non-rational, as long as we know why we want to apply whichever term we may apply.

After science and art—theology. It may seem odd to include theology in a list of factors tending towards the non-rational view of religion. Surely it is better regarded as a part of the non-rational view, rather than as something predisposing towards it? This is true; yet it is only one side of the truth. The teachings of particular theologians can also be perfectly properly presented as an influence tending towards the ever wider acceptance of the contemporary view of religion—one influence among others.

Karl Barth (b. 1886) is the obvious illustration here. Barth's teachings to the effect that Christianity is based on revelation alone and not on reason (see, e.g. Brunner and Barth, especially pp. 67–128) have certainly played a considerable part in providing backing for the contemporary view. These teachings have, incidentally, sometimes been misunderstood. Barth's irrationalist position has been criticized as inconsistent, on the grounds that Barth, while claiming that the Christian religion is based solely on revelation and not at all on reason, is at the same time inflicting on the public theological works of stupefying length whose writing clearly requires on the part of their author the exercise of considerable rational powers. But this criticism must, however reluctantly, be set aside as mistaken. It is true that Barth offers a highly systematic exposition of revelation. This is an indication that he thinks religion is rational, in the sense of rationally expressible. (Though, as it happens, he would not himself want to call religion 'rational'. Religion, he would claim, is 'above' rationality and non-rationality.) But this kind of rationality is very different from the kind of rationality that Barth certainly rejects: viz. the claim that religion has a rational basis; that is, that some central religious beliefs—particularly belief in God— are capable of being demonstrated by argument. There is no inconsistency in holding both these positions.

Barth is not the only twentieth-century theologian whose teachings have helped to produce the contemporary view of religion, but he is the dominant influence; such other theologians as Emil Brunner, Martin Buber, or Reinhold Niebuhr, are either not as wholehearted in their anti-rationalism or not as powerful in urging it.

Naturally, the influence of the theologians has been greater on religious believers than on sceptics, who are more likely to have reached the contemporary view through science or art, or, of course, in some quite other way than those that have been considered in this chapter. Although it is not easy to be certain in these matters it seems safe to say that the contribution of theology to the forming of the contemporary view has not been any less than that of science or art.

To set theology alongside science and art, as I have done in this chapter, helps to underline the fact that the contemporary view of religion is confined neither to believers nor to non-believers. At the same time, the fact that the contemporary view is shared by both the religious and the irreligious ought not of itself to excite too soon in men of goodwill hopes of a reconciliation between believer and sceptic. The contemporary view numbers among its supporters some very uneasy, and probably permanently uneasy, bedfellows. Any examination of the things that people mean by 'non-rational' is to be expected to bring out the differences between people's views rather than to show that after all there are no differences between people's views. 'The contemporary view' is no more than a convenient label, referring to a general kind of similarity. Such a label serves the purpose of superficially pasting over the cracks; but a mere label has no power to fill in cracks.

My aim so far has been a simple one. In the previous chapter I tried to say what the philosophy of religion is about, and singled out as its central theme the question: what is the place of reason in religion? In the present chapter I have called attention to what I take to be the distinctively contemporary answer to that question: there is no place for reason in religion (though this puts the answer rather more crudely than I have hitherto). In the chapter which now follows I attempt a more systematic, if brief, discussion of the expressions 'rational' and 'non-rational' as these are applied to religion: for to note the fact that people tend nowadays to characterize religion as non-rational does not of itself take us very far; this is uninformative in the absence of some sorting out of what they may mean when they so characterize it. A large part of my intention in the writing of these two opening chapters has, indeed, been to illustrate, in an unmethodical way, the extent to which 'non-rational', and, of course, 'rational', mean different things on different occasions of their use.

CHAPTER 3

'Rational' and 'Non-Rational'

IT IS natural to suppose that 'rational' on the one hand and 'non-rational' and 'irrational' taken together on the other stand in the relation of opposites. But this supposition is not borne out by even a superficial consideration of the way in which the words are commonly used. In some ideal language they might well stand in this simple, uncomplicated relationship; but we are concerned here with what these words mean in use and for the people who actually use them. For instance, 'He is a rational man' would, in some contexts, most naturally be countered by not 'He is irrational' but 'He is stupid, pig-headed'. Again, 'There must be some rational explanation' might be countered not by 'There must be some irrational explanation' but by the claim that there is no explanation at all. ('There must be some rational explanation' is usually only a strong way of saying, 'There must be some explanation'.)

Let us look at some of the variety of uses of these terms. There may be many other uses than those that I am about to mention; I make no claim that the list is complete. For the sake of simplicity I shall take 'rational' as the positive term, and 'non-rational' and 'irrational' as negatives—this is certainly what their form suggests—but a discussion aiming at greater completeness would need also to consider whether there may be cases where 'non-rational' or 'irrational' function as positives and 'rational' as a negative. We have already had occasion to note the different emotive forces of 'non-rational' and 'irrational', the one generally favourable, the other generally unfavourable, and nothing more need be said about this now; though it ought, perhaps, to be noted that 'irrational' may not always indicate an unfavourable emotive attitude. For to the Modern Protestant, influenced by Kierkegaard and as represented most consistently by Barth, religion is 'radically' irrational, in the sense that it is held to be neither rational nor non-rational but beyond the possibility of being either; and this 'irrationality' of religion is regarded as something to glory in. I shall concentrate upon uses of the terms that have some bearing upon religion; no notice at all will be taken of, for instance, the mathematical uses of 'rational' and 'irrational'.

'Rational', in appropriate contexts, may be used to mean one or more of the following (the natural opposite, where there is one, is put in brackets): 'sane' (insane), 'demonstrable as true' (demonstrable as false), 'capable of being expressed in meaningful statements' (incapable of being expressed in meaningful statements), 'true' (false), 'exists' (does not exist), 'clear-headed, unemotional' (emotional), 'likely, plausible' (unlikely, implausible), 'unparadoxical' (paradoxical), 'systematic, consistent' (unsystematic, inconsistent), 'scientific' (unscientific), 'matter-of-fact, down-to-earth' (remote, fantastic), etc. In a more limited religious or theological context 'rational theology' is opposed to 'revealed theology'; and 'rationalism' (in the sense of the anti-theistic movement that flourished more particularly in the nineteenth century) is opposed to 'religion'.

So as to impose some order on the complexity of the material, let us lay it down for our present purposes that 'rational' is used either (1) of *people* or (2) of whole *systems* of belief or behaviour or (3) of isolated *beliefs*.

(1) To say that a person is rational, or that he is irrational, may mean several things. It often seems to mean that he has a certain sort of character, which shows itself in his attitude to other people, to his surroundings in general, to knowledge or claims to knowledge. 'Man is a rational animal.' True. But some men are more rational than others. The man who is singled out by this epithet is the man who is level-headed, given to weighing things up judiciously, open to persuasion, not unduly swayed by his

emotions, and so on. (I am not suggesting that this is always what it means.) The rational man is not necessarily a very intelligent man (though he may be), and not necessarily a well-informed man. In calling a man 'rational' we commonly, though not necessarily, mean to praise him, which seems to imply that we suppose being rational (in this sense) to be something that is within the power of at least some men to achieve, as being intelligent perhaps is not.

(2) A system of belief or behaviour may be called rational or irrational. We have seen examples of this earlier. Religion, considered in this way, is described as rational—or as irrational, depending on your point of view. The schizophrenic is called irrational. Science may be described as rational, by scientists, in contrast to pre-scientific or unscientific systems of belief or kinds of procedure. Some movements in art may be described by some laymen as irrational.

Reasons will have to be given, of course, to back up such judgements; and in the giving of reasons more specific features of the systems in question will be touched upon. The blanket praise or dispraise expressed in the judgement 'X is rational' or 'X is irrational', or the more neutral assessment expressed in 'X is non-rational', does not convey very much until these specific features have been laid bare. Even then discussion may not get very far; for there is no necessary relation of entailment between being such-and-such a specific feature of religion, schizophrenia, science, or whatever it may be, and being rational or irrational. It might, for instance, be held by one man that religion as a whole is irrational because religious beliefs, or the most important of them, are accepted on authority, and the acceptance of anything on authority is an irrational procedure. But this might be denied by another, who holds that although in the case of some other sets of beliefs it would be irrational to accept them on authority alone, religion is different; religion being what it is, it would be irrational to insist on any ground *other than* authority for accepting these beliefs. In a sense, both men are justified. Certainly, religion is irrational, if accepting things on authority is in general irrational, and if it is agreed—as it must be—that religion involves accepting some things on authority. But the link between being accepted on authority and being irrational is not a clear one; and anyone who wishes to argue for the rationality of religion has a perfect right to try, if he likes, to make out a case for the acceptance of things on authority being in general, or in particular cases, a rational procedure.

(3) My third heading may seem to be only the second all over again; but this is not so. It is appropriate to distinguish particular beliefs from systems of belief or behaviour, if only because 'rational' and 'irrational' (or 'non-rational') are more naturally applied to the latter type of case than to the former. 'Religion is irrational', 'Science is rational': these have a more familiar ring than would a similar statement about some particular belief. Indeed, so comparatively uncommon is the latter kind of use of 'rational' and 'irrational' that it is difficult to find a case which, taken out of context and set down here for an example, would not look somewhat unnatural. The ascription of rationality or irrationality is more appropriately made to general beliefs than to particular ones, or to the grounds of belief than to particular beliefs. 'It is irrational to accept things on mere authority', we might say. We are much less likely to say, 'It is irrational to believe that today is Tuesday', or even, 'It is irrational to believe that $2+2 = 5$'. A statement like, 'It is irrational to believe that the earth is flat', though it may look as if it is a statement about a particular belief, is really about a whole network of beliefs—all the things that would be entailed by the flatness of the earth.

To call a belief 'rational' or 'irrational' is often to do something other than calling it 'true' or 'false'; though it may well be to do this also. It is often to suggest that it does, or does not, fit into a system of beliefs: hence the priority of my second heading over the third. There is nothing in the least surprising about this. It is no more than one would expect. 'Rational' and 'irrational' have a fairly close affinity with 'logical' and 'illogical' (though the two sets of terms are not interchangeable), and are often used to mean something like 'consistent' or 'inconsistent'. 'It is irrational to believe that Jesus was raised from the dead', the sceptic may say; meaning by this that this belief is inconsistent with all that we know and believe about death and human bodies.

Within a given system of belief or behaviour a particular item may be called rational or irrational, implying that it does or does not 'fit into' that system. A system of belief or behaviour may itself be called rational or irrational, implying either that it is, as a whole, internally consistent or inconsistent, or, sometimes, that it does or does not fit in with other systems. This is the difference between the third and the second of my three headings. The difference is not, in practice, as clear-cut as this. Particular parts of a system may well be seized upon with the intention of showing them to be inconsistent not with the other items of the same system but with items in another system. The believer and the sceptic will want to make rather different connexions when they consider 'Jesus was raised from the dead'.

This has the perhaps curious-sounding consequence that a belief or a system of beliefs may sometimes be said to be rational but false, irrational but true. (The same point can be made about 'consistent' and 'inconsistent'.) From the point of view of another system, B, a given system, A, or an item in it, may seem irrational; and in calling it this the upholder of system B probably means to say that it is false. But the upholder of system A is free to agree that his system, or some particular belief in it, is irrational, in the sense that it is inconsistent with system B, which we may suppose to be that adhered to by the majority, while refusing to agree that it is therefore false. (Modern Protestantism, while itself insisting on the irrationality of religion, is far from coupling this with the belief that religion is false: though, admittedly, the sense of 'irrationality' here—'radical irrationality'—is, as noted earlier, a somewhat special one, and one that needs strictly to be distinguished from the sense just referred to.)

As far as religion is concerned, the second and third of the three uses are more important than the first. That is not to say that it is never appropriate to say things like, 'The religious believer— or that individual in so far as he is a religious believer—is rational/ irrational', or, 'Christians are as rational as anyone else', etc. But it seems more appropriate to use the words in contexts like 'Religion is irrational', or 'Belief in a Virgin Birth is irrational'. It is significant that the examples that come naturally to mind are those using 'irrational' rather than 'rational'. This illustrates the perhaps obvious fact that Christians (or rather, some Christians; for we must except certain modern Protestants) only find it necessary to argue for the rationality of their religion when sceptics begin to argue for its irrationality. On the whole, men assume the 'rationality' of what they believe in; they do not feel any need to make this explicit to themselves by the use of the word 'rational' itself. Indeed, to come to use such a word at all is already perhaps to have admitted—it may be, hardly consciously—that there is a fairly strong case on the other side.

But, as I have already said, what really matters is not the mere assertion that religion is rational or that it is irrational. What matters is what exactly 'rational' or 'irrational' are being used to mean. Or, as I expressed it earlier, what matters is the reasons for the application of these words. These reasons are various; and some of the chief ones are to be discussed in the following chapters.

Consider first the view that religion is rational. Traditionally the case for the rationality of religion was made to rest mainly on the standard arguments for the existence of God—arguments that once took up a great deal of space in books on the philosophy of religion, but that have more recently, for a variety of reasons, been pushed rather into the background. I think this relegation is undeserved, and in the present book I have given them what may seem to some readers a prominence as undue as it is old-fashioned. From this point of view, to say that religion is rational amounts to the claim that the existence of God can be proved. It may well be that to have proved the existence of God—assuming that this can be done, and it would be widely held nowadays that it cannot—would not be to have proved very much: there is more to religion than belief in God. This is true; but it must be remembered that, according to the usual traditional view in these matters, reason goes hand-in-hand with revelation. Traditionally, to hold that religion is rational is not to hold that every detail of it is capable of being established by argument, but rather that its centre, which has generally been held to be the existence of a Supreme Being with a particular set of attributes, can be so established, as a basis on which revelation, or faith, may then build up the rest.

Although attempts to provide a rational basis for religion have

typically taken the form of attempts to prove the existence of
God they have not done so invariably. Joseph Butler (1692–1752)
in his *Analogy of Religion* (1736), written in an endeavour to meet
the Deists of his day on their own ground—to out-rationalize the
rationalists—assumes the existence of God, and instead argues
that specifically Christian beliefs, such as the belief that God has
provided a Mediator between himself and man, are, as far as
rationality or irrationality are concerned, on a level with those
of natural religion. The beliefs for whose rationality he thus
obliquely argues are in fact those that in the usual traditional
view are regarded as dependent on revelation and as beyond the
competence of reason to establish.

Another sense in which religion may be held to be rational is
one which, in the form which follows at any rate, has not occurred
to supporters of religion until recently. This is because it is really
the denial of a particular form of the view that religion is *ir*-
rational which has itself only recently been put forward.
It is a view that springs naturally out of twentieth-century
developments in philosophy, and that could not have been arrived
at without them—could not, in the sense that it depends upon an
idiom that philosophers in earlier ages did not use. This is the
view that religion is rational because expressible in a set of
meaningful assertions, and is the denial of the view that religion
is irrational because religious utterances are not genuine assertions. The issue here is a somewhat technical one, and will be
made clearer in Chapter 12.

Let us turn from forms of the view that religion is rational to
forms of the view that it is irrational.

One of these has just been referred to—that what seem to be
assertions in religion are not genuine assertions at all.

Another—Freud's—has also been mentioned already: religion
is irrational in the sense that it is the product of wish-fulfilment.
Freud is not the only psychologist who has concerned himself
with religion, and we shall in a later chapter be considering more
fully the implications not only of Freud's view but also of one
which stands at the opposite extreme from his, and which would
regard religion as something into which men may be 'conditioned'.

The view that regards religion as irrational on the grounds

that it involves taking things on authority has also been mentioned. Then there is the view that it is irrational because it is 'unscientific', or non-empirical, or because it deals in unverifiable supernatural causes (or alleged causes). Again, particular religious doctrines are attacked as being inconsistent with fact—the chief case in point being sufficiently indicated by the phrase 'the problem of evil'. We have already noted the Modern Protestant view that religion is radically irrational, that religion is 'beyond' rationality and non-rationality, that it is inappropriate to apply such categories, whether positive or negative, to it at all. I do not propose to discuss this further, but in the chapters that follow most of the other views mentioned above will be discussed more fully. On the whole, as I have written earlier, the view that religion is *ir*rational has had the best of it in recent years. I have called it the contemporary view. We may hope to see more clearly in later chapters into the complexity of the forms that it takes.

In the next three chapters I discuss the best known of the traditional arguments for the existence of God, the Ontological Argument (in Chapter 4), the Cosmological Argument (in Chapter 5), and the Teleological Argument or Argument from Design (in Chapter 6).

The Ontological Argument

SAINT Anselm (1033–1109) was born at Aosta in Piedmont, the son of a nobleman; entered the Benedictine abbey of Bec in Normandy where he rose to be abbot; and in 1093 was made, against his will, Archbishop of Canterbury in succession to Lanfranc, his former teacher. Anselm was the originator of the Ontological Argument, which, although attacked both immediately and since, has often been revived and has never ceased to exercise fascination even on those who have felt bound to reject it.

The Ontological Argument was not Anselm's first attempt at proving the existence of God. Earlier he had developed an argument, in his *Monologion*, which we will not consider here but which was rather like that later put forward by St. Thomas Aquinas (1224–74) as the fourth of his Five Ways. But the argument of the *Monologion* did not satisfy Anselm; for precisely the reasons for which the Five Ways did satisfy Aquinas. (Aquinas considered himself to be greatly at variance with Anselm in his view about the conditions that would need to be met by an acceptable argument for the existence of God. I hope to show later that the difference between the two men is not as great as Aquinas thought.) Anselm then sought about for a line of reasoning that would be utterly simple and not, as that of the *Monologion* had been, an elaborate complex of complementary arguments; and that would not involve, as that had done, arguing to God from his creatures. He did not easily find what he wanted; but, a year or so later, the argument that by then he had almost despaired of ever discovering, presented itself to him. He offered it to the world in a work called *Proslogion* (or Address).

Before we state and examine the Ontological Argument itself some remarks must be made about Anselm's intentions; for these are sometimes misunderstood. It is, fortunately, not hard to establish what was in his mind. The most striking feature of the *Proslogion* is the fact that most of it is written in the form of an address *to God*. Anselm does not typically say, 'God is . . .'. He says, 'Thou, God, art . . .'. This is of considerable importance. Anselm's *Proslogion* is not a dispassionate philosophical treatise, written by an open-minded man who is trying to see whether it is possible to prove, not merely to others but to himself, that God exists. It is a prayer, in places an impassioned prayer, written by a devout believer in God, addressed to God, and punctuated by appeals for divine help. Anselm is not at all doubtful whether there is a God. His aim in looking for a rational demonstration of God's existence is not to convince himself that God exists, but rather (he claims) that he may come to *understand* more fully what he in any case already *believes*. He prefaces his statement of the Argument itself with the famous sentence: 'I do not seek to understand in order that I may believe, but I believe in order that I may understand (*credo, ut intelligam*)'. He adds: 'For this also I believe, that unless I believe I shall not understand'.

This attitude lying behind Anselm's presentation of the Ontological Argument is as important as the Argument itself. 'I believe in order that I may understand . . . . Unless I believe I shall not understand'. His significance lies not least in the clarity with which he saw this attitude in himself and not merely admitted it but stressed its indispensability.

There is room for discussion about what exactly Anselm meant by *credo ut intelligam*, or by the phrase *fides quaerens intellectum* (faith seeking understanding) which had been his original title for the *Proslogion*. But it is at least safe to say that his position is a good deal stronger than some others that may at first sight appear to be the same. For instance, F. H. Bradley wrote: 'Metaphysics is the finding of bad reasons for what we believe upon instinct, but to find these reasons is no less an instinct' (Bradley, p. xii). What is important for our present purposes in Bradley's aphorism is the calling to our attention of a particular order in events: first the belief, and only then the reasons. The remark is more striking than entirely true. But it is true to a large extent; and true not only of metaphysics or of natural theology. It is true also of science; for the scientist very often (some would say, always) gets his hypotheses first and looks for convincing evidence afterwards. In many fields of inquiry, indeed, belief may be said to come first and argument second. This is not to say that beliefs always come unpreceded by reasons of any kind; for this, of course, is not so. The point is rather that people may and do frequently hold beliefs without being sure on what grounds they hold them; or if they are sure on what grounds they hold them, without having subjected those grounds to any close scrutiny. The reasons for which people as a matter of fact hold beliefs is one thing: the question what would be *good* reasons for those beliefs is another. (This point underlay my second chapter, in which I noted some of the things that have as a matter of fact predisposed people to the non-rational view of religion, but suspended any judgement on their adequacy as grounds for that view.) Belief, then, may come first: the search for reasons, in the sense of good reasons, is likely to come only later.

But this is not what Anselm is saying; and we can see more clearly what it is that he is saying when we contrast his view with that just outlined. He is not saying simply that, in the case of God, we tend as a matter of fact to believe first and look for reasons afterwards. He is saying that *unless* we first believe in God we shall never understand adequately what is meant by belief in God. By 'believe' he does not mean merely 'entertain as likely', which is what a scientist may be said to be doing with his hypothesis before he seeks support for it, but 'believe' in a stronger, 'religious', sense, where 'to believe' may be paraphrased by 'to commit oneself in faith'. Commitment to God Anselm sees as a necessary preliminary to understanding God—understanding both his existence and his nature.

Anselm's position is certainly, then, stronger than that which we have got out of the quotation from Bradley. It is also in an important way quite different from it. Bradley, as I am interpreting him, is saying merely that the acceptance of a belief as a matter of fact often precedes the finding of reasons for it. A stronger view than this, but still recognizably a view of the same kind, would be that prior commitment to a belief is a necessary condition of the discovery of reasons for it. This is a view that one might, but wrongly, be tempted to attribute to Anselm. But Anselm does not, in fact, say that unless you first believe in God you will never be able to find reasons for belief in him. Not at all. The atheist is as able as the theist to follow the logic of an argument for the existence of God—like Anselm's own Ontological Argument—and Anselm is far from denying this. No; he is not asserting that faith is a necessary condition of the discovery, the following, or even the accepting, of reasons for belief in God. He is asserting that it is a necessary condition of understanding God, of understanding what the believer believes—understanding the existence and nature of God in, as far as the limitations of human comprehension allow, its full meaning.

On the question of the connexion between belief and reasons or arguments Anselm's position may perhaps be usefully explained by invoking ideas made familiar by John Henry Newman (1801–90) in his *Grammar of Assent*. Inferences are hypothetical. We may acknowledge that the conclusion of an argument follows validly from its premisses; but we are not thereby bound to assent to that conclusion. It may be that we consider the premisses false, or perhaps only possibly but not certainly true. In such a case, the fact that the conclusion is entailed by the premisses cannot lead us to say definitely that it is true. In some such way as this it is possible for someone to claim that Anselm's Ontological Argument is valid and yet withhold his assent to its conclusion. It is often assumed that the theistic arguments, if they are valid at all, ought to have equal power to convince both believer and non-believer. But Anselm does not suppose that his Ontological Argument will convert the sceptic: it is the person who believes in God already who can profit from it.

This attitude of Anselm's may seem to be in conflict with his own famous reference to the 'fool' who 'hath said in his heart "There is no God" ' (Psalm xiv, 1). Of the fool—i.e. the atheist—Anselm says that even he has the idea of God in his understanding; for the fool understands what is meant by the word 'God', even though he does not understand that God exists. Does this then mean that it is possible to have understanding of God without belief in God? An examination of what Anselm says about the fool will reveal that there is no real conflict here. He distinguishes two senses in which we may think of a thing. We may think of it (he says in Chapter IV of the *Proslogion*) merely in the sense that we think of the word that signifies it. We may, on the other hand, think of it in the sense that we really understand the thing itself. The atheist, in denying God, although he must be thinking of God in order to deny him, can only, Anselm believes, be thinking of him in the first sense. So there is no conflict between having God in the understanding and denying God. (It may be doubted whether Anselm's first kind of 'thinking of' is really a kind of 'thinking of' at all. But whatever one calls it, the situation he is referring to is real enough.)

For Anselm, conviction of the existence of God is at all times a matter of faith. Reason alone can never provide it. Nevertheless, reason can strengthen and confirm faith. He writes, when he has come to the end of the statement of the Argument, that he now understands by God's light what formerly he believed by God's gift, and then he significantly seems to go on to imply that if he now found himself wanting not to believe in God this would be difficult; for the insight into the necessary existence of God that he has received through the Argument would draw him back to belief.

Anselm's view that belief precedes understanding can hardly be intended to mean that a man may believe something without understanding it at all; for what then would he be believing? Belief and understanding must to some extent go together. Anselm, it seems, is saying that full understanding of God (within human limits) may come only to the man who believes in God; but clearly some understanding of God (incomplete or even in part mistaken) must always be involved in belief.

There is a very natural objection to Anselm's position that must be dealt with. To say that an argument for the existence of God is of value only to someone who is already a believer in him may seem tantamount to saying that it is of no value at all. For the believer in God is not in need of proof: and the person who may be felt to need a proof—the sceptic—is, it seems, to be ruled out by his very scepticism from any possibility of profiting from the argument; otherwise, that is, than through the mental exercise the following of the argument may afford him. But this criticism rests on a misunderstanding. It is essential to realize that Anselm did not think of his Ontological Argument purely as a proof of God's existence. Its function is indeed not so much to prove that God exists as to help the believer to understand what he means when he asserts that God exists. By later writers the Ontological Argument has certainly sometimes been put forward with the claim that it is a proof valid for believer and sceptic alike; but this is not how Anselm himself intended it. He saw it as an instrument designed to make clearer the already-held notion of divine existence, rather than to prove it.

Anselm is, paradoxically, both a rationalist and a mystic. On the one hand, he is driven by the urge to understand his Christian faith. To this end he devises many rational arguments, both in the *Proslogion* and in his other works. Yet on the other hand, his method of writing is such that the *Proslogion* has been said to be mystical theology rather than philosophy; and it has been suggested that the 'understanding' at which he aims is not philosophical but mystical—the kind of understanding that can be identified with union with God in contemplation. It is in this double aspect—as mystic and philosopher—that Anselm's significance lies. In him we see the reflection of St. Augustine, and, behind Augustine, that of Plato. Clearly, his supposition (to generalize it) that only the Christian believer can hope to understand Christian beliefs is of the greatest consequence. If we accept it, much that has been written subsequently by less committed philosophers will have to be rejected as missing the point.

After these necessary preliminaries, let us look at Anselm's Ontological Argument itself.

We may conveniently express the line of thought followed by Anselm in Chapters II and III of the *Proslogion* in three steps.

1. *Definition*. He begins by defining God. 'Thou art a being than which none greater can be conceived.' It is clear, he says, that the idea of God, as such a being, exists in (some) men's minds. So God exists in the understanding. The question is whether he

exists in reality. (It is usual to say that Anselm begins with a definition of God, and I have followed convention by saying this myself; but it should be noted that this 'definition' is a definition of a rather special sort. It is exceedingly general and formal— some might say, vague—and this, as I hope to show, is a fact of considerable importance in the defence of Anselm against criticism.)

2. *Reductio ad absurdum.* Assume that God does not exist in reality but only in the understanding. But if this is so then God is not, as defined, a being than which none greater can be conceived. For you could conceive of a being (otherwise the same) that existed also in reality, and such a being would be greater than a being that existed only in the understanding. So God, the being than which none greater can be conceived, would then be a being than which a greater *can* be conceived. And this is absurd. So the initial assumption is false; that is, it is false that God exists in the understanding only and not in reality. Therefore God does exist in reality as well as in the understanding.

3. *Necessary existence.* Furthermore, a being that cannot be thought of as not existing is greater than a being that can be thought of as not existing. If God could be thought of as not existing he would not be as great as a being that cannot be thought of as not existing. In other words, there is a contradiction in saying both that God is a being than which none greater can be conceived and that God might not exist. 'Thou so truly art, O Lord my God, that thou canst not be thought of as not existing.'

I want to call attention at the outset to two things about this argument. The first is what we may call its 'purity'. As we have already noted, Anselm's intention was to arrive at a proof of God that would be single, simple, not a complex of inter-related arguments; and that would prove God *from God himself* and not by any type of causal reasoning from creatures to Creator. The Ontological Argument does have these intended properties: and to this extent it is different from other theistic arguments. The purity—that seems the right word—of Anselm's intentions is there to be acknowledged. He wanted a proof of God that would not make knowledge of God depend on anything other than God himself. Any element of the empirical in the proof (we may suppose him thinking) would involve a kind of demeaning of God. The definition of God from which he begins is a purely formal one. The apparently empirical nature of the reference to the idea of God as existing *in men's minds* is only superficially so: it is the concept or idea itself of God from which he really starts, not from the fact of the possession of this idea by men. (We may contrast with this Descartes's First Proof, to be discussed in the next chapter, which also begins, but with quite a different emphasis, from the idea of God.) Anselm wanted to start from God quite explicitly, as well as to finish with God. The common charge that theistic arguments assume what they are supposed to prove can obviously especially easily be brought against Anselm. He makes no concealment of the fact that in his beginning is his end: he is perfectly aware of what he is doing.

The other important feature of the Argument is its reliance on the logical Principle (or 'Law') of Contradiction; as can be seen in the second of the three steps just outlined. This gives it a force not always possessed by theistic arguments, which tend to be built around metaphysical, or even empirical, principles that may themselves need arguing for, whereas the Principle of Contradiction would generally be supposed not to need this.

These two features are obviously closely related to each other: the second could be presented as being merely one aspect of the first. They go a long way towards explaining why the Ontological Argument has continued to fascinate philosophers.

It should be borne in mind that Anselm's, although the first, is not the only formulation of the Ontological Argument. Criticisms are often brought against something called *the* Ontological Argument; and, for that matter, the argument itself, as are the other theistic arguments, is sometimes presented as if it existed in its own right apart from the formulations of individual philosophers. This procedure is valid enough within limits, but there are obvious drawbacks to it. I do not deny that there is something that can legitimately be called *the* Ontological Argument, and I do not deny that there are what can equally legitimately be called *the* objections to the Ontological Argument. At the same time we must not forget that there are different versions of it. I am concentrating here on Anselm's, as being not only the original version but also, I think, the subtlest; but the argument appears also in St. Bonaventure (1221–74), in Descartes (1596–1650), in Spinoza (1632–77), in Leibniz (1646–1716), in Hegel, and in other writers. Not all criticisms of the argument apply with equal force to all versions of it. In particular, criticisms are sometimes brought against Anselm that do not really apply to his version of the Ontological Argument, though they may apply to other versions. Let us now consider some of these criticisms.

(1) Even the foolish man who says there is no God understands what is meant by 'God', Anselm says. This is just what might be doubted by some people at the present time. As they see it, the issue about belief in God is not: Does God exist or does he not? It is rather: What does 'God' mean? Some present-day philosophers would refuse to be classified as theists, atheists, or agnostics, in the way people in the nineteenth century were happy to classify themselves and each other. Only when the problem of the meaning of 'God' is settled to their satisfaction will they agree to be classified in this way, and this problem for some is far from settled. They are neither theists nor atheists, for they do not know what they would be assenting to if they said they were theists or what they would be denying if they said they were atheists; equally, they are not agnostics, for the agnostic is traditionally the man who cannot make up his mind which way to take, whereas the type of thinker that I have in mind is not clear about what ways there are, and this is a more fundamental doubt.

The reference to the 'fool' needs, of course, to be taken in conjunction with the point that we have already had occasion to notice about the two senses in which Anselm believes we may think of something. There is no particular problem about the weaker of the two senses—where to think of a thing is, as Anselm holds, merely to think of the word that signifies it. But, in the case of God, the stronger sense—where to think of a thing is to understand the very thing itself—does give rise to difficulty.

(2) What, in fact, is meant by the concept of God? We are

concerned here with what Anselm thought it meant, and he himself, it is clear, had no difficulty in understanding it. I have already called attention to the fact that the definition from which he begins is a purely formal one—that is, it contains no specific reference to any of God's attributes, but rather offers a kind of framework into which his attributes can later be fitted. Obviously, the more formal a definition is, the less it is open to criticism. But, equally, the more formal, the less informative. Is someone who is trying to discover the meaning of the concept of God likely to consider his search at an end when he is told that God is a being than which none greater can be conceived? Hardly. Yet Anselm was satisfied with this (as far as getting a starting point for the Ontological Argument is concerned) as an account of what the concept of God means. Or, rather, not with this alone; for we need to include an explicit reference to God's necessary existence. For although Anselm does not mention necessary existence at the start, it is a vital part of his argument, an argument which, as we have already noted, can be regarded as a device for drawing out and explaining what the concept of God means. Let us say, then, that as far as Anselm was concerned, an adequate initial account of the meaning of the concept of God can be given in the following terms: God is the only being to whom one can truth-fully say, 'Thou art a being than which none greater can be conceived' and (what in his opinion follows from this) 'Thou canst not be conceived not to be'. On the face of it, this seems accept-able. But let us look further at the general line of criticism which aims to cast doubt on the meaningfulness of 'God'; for although Anselm thought that the concept of God is meaningful and that (up to a point) he understood its meaning, some other thinkers have been far from willing to follow him in this.

(3) It is often argued either (*a*) that the concept of God is, or (*b*) that it may be, meaningless—for instance, because it is self-contradictory—and that consequently there can be no valid argument that takes this concept as its starting point.

(*a*) Consider the first half of this criticism. What is meant by saying that the concept of God is meaningless? (i) Sometimes what is meant is that there are attributes or properties of God that do not, at least *prima facie*, cohere; for example, perfect mercy and perfect justice (a perfectly merciful being would forgive all wrongdoing; a perfectly just being would punish all wrongdoing). Admittedly, interpretations of such terms as these can be arrived at on which the appearance of conflict is made to vanish. Anselm has a lot to say himself about this particular difficulty in Chapters IX–XI of the *Proslogion*. Nevertheless, the fact that as words like 'merciful' and 'just' are commonly used there certainly does seem to be a conflict between perfect mercy and perfect justice is a significant one. (ii) Another form of the criticism is as follows. Not all attributes admit of being maximized. It seems that there can be no intrinsic maxima of, for example, love or wisdom. (Consider an example from a different field. There is nothing to which the expression 'greatest natural integer' applies. In contrast, it would be generally held that there is a maximum degree of probability, namely $1/1$.) As the attributes of God include some that do not possess intrinsic maxima, the notion of God as a being than which none greater can be conceived is clearly meaningless. (See on this, Broad, p. 179.) This objection, again, can be evaded—this time by interpreting 'love', 'wisdom', etc., to mean love, wisdom, etc., of a special divine kind rather than love, wisdom, etc., in the highest degree. But then it is difficult to see how this kind of love, wisdom, etc., is commensurate with love, wisdom, etc., in the ordinary sense; and hence it is still difficult to see what can be meant by 'greater' or 'greatest' here. (iii) Yet another form of the objection consists in saying that the notion of a necessarily existing being is meaningless. Existence, it would be claimed, is such that any being that can be thought of as existing can equally well be thought of as not existing. I shall postpone discussion of this last point until later in the chapter; but points (i) and (ii) I shall deal with now.

The objection we are considering, in both the forms (i) and (ii), depends, it seems to me, on a misunderstanding of Anselm's argument. His choice of a purely formal definition as his starting point is surely entirely deliberate. Anselm, by excluding any reference to the properties of God, unless necessary existence is a property, covers himself against charges (i) and (ii). If no properties at all have been mentioned, then clearly no mutually incompatible properties have been mentioned. Equally, if no properties at all have been mentioned, no questions about what properties do and what do not admit of being maximized can be relevant.

This defence of Anselm might itself be objected to. No properties are mentioned; that is true: but, we may imagine Anselm's critics saying, properties are implied. To give any real meaning to the notion of a being than which none greater can be conceived do we not need to 'cash' it in terms of specific properties? Do we not need to understand it as meaning: God is a being than which none greater *in respect of love, wisdom, power, mercy, etc.* can be conceived? There is some justice in this rejoinder. As a matter of historical fact Anselm almost certainly must have arrived at his formal definition of God by abstracting from his personal belief in God as possessing certain properties in superlative degree—the properties, in fact, that he goes on to enumerate and discuss in the chapters of the *Proslogion* following those in which he states the Ontological Argument. It seems to me, though, that however it may have been arrived at, Anselm's definition logically stands on its own feet. Necessary existence he does seem to think is implied by it, or even to be a part of it; but no (other) particular properties are so implied.

(*b*) The other half of the present objection can be dealt with more briefly. It is sometimes charged against Anselm not that his definition of God *is* meaningless but merely that it *may be* so. The force of this is to suggest that the onus is on Anselm to prove that it is not, while the critic sits safely back without committing himself. Leibniz, and to some extent Descartes, accepted this challenge, and tried to show that there is no contradiction in the idea of God. Now, it may well be that Descartes, who thought he had a clear and distinct idea of God, can legitimately be challenged to show that his idea of God is indeed not self-contradictory; for on the face of it that finite minds should have a clear and distinct idea of an Infinite Being seems unlikely. But Anselm makes no such claim. He hopes 'in some measure' to understand. He does not, like Descartes, maintain that what we conceive clearly and distinctly is true, and that we conceive God clearly and distinctly. His idea of God, general and formal as it is, commits him to so little that the onus of proof of contradictoriness or non-contradictoriness may, I think, reasonably be said to be on his opponents, not on him.

Before I leave this subject there is something else that ought to be said. The objection that we have been considering, in both its halves, (*a*) and (*b*), seems altogether more serious when it is levelled against Anselm's Argument in isolation than when it is levelled against it in its context. We must remember that Anselm was writing for his fellow-theologians, with whom he held in common a highly complex system of beliefs. It is true that the notion of a being than which none greater can be conceived is one that ultimately needs interpretation, but he is tacitly assuming a particular interpretation of it. The phrase taken out of its context in his mind and considered simply as a set of words is certainly puzzling. What would the isolated phrase 'a being than which none greater can be conceived' most naturally suggest to someone who had never read, or even heard of, Anselm? It might well suggest something like, 'a being than which none greater in respect of size (i.e. none *bigger*) can be conceived'. This is certainly not what Anselm meant. Our imaginary questioner, again, might well wonder whether there may not be more than one being answering to this definition. This, too, is not what Anselm thought. Now Anselm, as it happens, has already considered the latter point and given his answer to it in the *Monologion*; and he implies an answer to the former point by what he says in the later chapters of the *Proslogion*. Anselm, then, is aware that there are difficulties of meaning involved in a phrase like 'a being than which none greater can be conceived'. To give the impression that, unlike Descartes or Leibniz, he simply does not see such difficulties would be quite wrong. His recognition of them is as unclouded as theirs, and his attempt to answer them as thorough. Where he differs from Descartes and Leibniz—in particular from Leibniz—is in not making his argument itself depend on an explicit demonstration that the idea of God is not self-contradictory. As I have said already, the argument logically stands on its own feet and depends simply upon a completely general and formal definition of God. The recognition of the argument's self-sufficiency need not prevent us from acknowledging at the same time that Anselm himself is well aware both that his formal definition must at some stage be filled out ('greater' is an incomplete predicate, and must certainly at some point be limited), and that some of the commonly accepted divine attributes are at least *prima facie* mutually incompatible. Perhaps, then, it is not unreasonable in the circumstances to suggest that when he uses the phrase 'a being than which none greater can be conceived' he should be understood as meaning, 'a being than which none greater in respect of non-mutually-incompatible attributes can be conceived'.

In short, then, to the objection often made that only if the concept of God is self-consistent can Anselm's Ontological Argument work, the proper answer is that Anselm knows this very well, that he does indeed think that the concept of God is self-consistent, and that he has argued elsewhere at length for its self-consistency. His Ontological Argument begins on the assumption that the concept of God is self-consistent; but this is no unthinking assumption; it is a considered opinion for which he is prepared to argue in the proper place. Of course, it remains true that his arguments might be judged to be bad ones; though they seem to me to be sound enough. I am concerned at present to defend him against the charge of having overlooked an obvious objection to his position.

As I have been attempting in the last few pages to offer a defence of Anselm's argument, against one common type of criticism, I ought perhaps to say plainly now that I do not think the argument is a valid one. My claim will in the end be merely that it is not to be disposed of with as much ease as some have thought.

(4) On its publication Anselm's Argument was attacked by Gaunilo, a monk of Marmoutier (near Tours). Gaunilo's argument was directed against the way in which Anselm moves from thought to reality. From the mere idea of God, God's existence can never be deduced, Gaunilo claims; and he makes his point with the help of the following illustration. Let us suppose a perfect island—an island without owner or inhabitant and abundant beyond all inhabited lands in everything that might be appropriated as wealth. The idea of such an island is perfectly meaningful. Suppose someone now to argue: 'You cannot doubt

4]   THE ONTOLOGICAL ARGUMENT   39

that this island exists not merely in the understanding but in reality; for it is more excellent to be in reality than in the understanding alone, and unless this island exists in reality another island which does exist in reality would be more excellent than it, so that what we have begun by defining as the most perfect of islands would, after all, not be the most perfect of islands'. If, says Gaunilo, someone were to argue in this way, we should doubt whether he or we were the more foolish—he for offering the argument (unless he were joking) or we for accepting it (if we did).

Anselm in his reply to Gaunilo claims that God is a special case. This seems to me, as far as it goes, a perfectly adequate reply to the objection. The argument about the island would indeed be invalid, but it does not follow that the argument about God is invalid. In effect, what Anselm is saying is that a perfect island is only an *island* than which none greater can be conceived, but God is a *being* than which none greater can be conceived. To put it in positive rather than comparative terms, a perfect island is only the greatest conceivable of its kind, but God is the greatest conceivable in an absolute sense. God cannot be thought of as non-existent. This, the main point of Anselm's reply to Gaunilo, is brought out clearly in his reaction to a suggestion of the latter's to the effect that Anselm ought not to have said that God's non-existence cannot be conceived but that it cannot be understood (or known). Anselm will have none of this; and his reason for rejecting it is precisely that this would destroy the uniqueness of God. It is true of *everything* that actually exists that it cannot be *known* as not existing; for we cannot 'know' what is not the case. God is far from being unique in this respect. But it is certainly not true of everything that it cannot be *conceived* as not existing. Indeed, generally speaking, whatever exists can be conceived as not existing. There is point, then, in claiming that God is an exception to this; and just this is the claim that Anselm makes. God, says Anselm, is the only being which cannot be conceived as not existing; except, of course, in the superficial sense in which the 'fool' supposes him not to exist.

(5) It has been claimed that on Anselm's view 'God exists' must be analytic. If existence is part of the very meaning of

D

'God', then to say that God exists is merely to call attention to the meaning of a word, not to give information about a matter of non-linguistic fact. To put it a little differently, it is objected that on Anselm's view it is seen to be self-evident that God exists. St. Thomas Aquinas objected that it is not self-evident that God exists: God's essence no doubt does involve his existence; but we cannot know this.

A modern Thomist, Professor E. L. Mascall, while admitting that Anselm, unlike Descartes, does not claim to have a clear and distinct idea of God, notes that he nevertheless gives as the starting point of his Argument a definition of God. And this, Professor Mascall claims, following Aquinas, is just what we cannot start from. 'Any ontological argument demands, as the condition of its construction, that we shall have a knowledge of God's nature which the very notion of God denies us' (Mascall (2), p. 27). But this criticism, though it has some force against Descartes, has none against Anselm. Anselm's argument starts from something that can only by courtesy—or, indeed, only in error—be called knowledge of the nature or essence of God. As Professor Mascall himself says, Anselm does not claim to have a clear and distinct idea of God. He is constantly insistent on the limitations of human knowledge of God. To say of God that he is a being than which none greater can be conceived, and that he cannot be conceived not to be, is really to say very little; and the absence of reference to specific properties indicates the extent to which in his Ontological Argument for God's existence Anselm is assuming the distance between God and man. Note the paradoxical phrase in the above quotation from Professor Mascall: 'a knowledge of God's nature which the very notion of God denies us'. Professor Mascall is referring to the notion of God as transcendent. But to have the notion of God as transcendent, far from excluding knowledge of God's nature is itself to know something of God's nature. Admittedly, to know of God only that he is transcendent would not be to know very much. But neither is to know of him that he is a being than which none greater can be conceived to know very much. The apparent strength of the Thomist attack on the 'essentialism' of Anselm depends on a failure to see the significance of the purely formal character of Anselm's definition of God. Anselm's statement is no more and no less a statement about the essence of God than is the statement 'God is transcendent' which lies behind the Thomist attack on him.

To put the point again slightly differently. Aquinas, at any rate as his position is represented by followers like Mascall, rejects Anselm's Ontological Argument on the grounds that it starts from the wrong end. Anselm, such Thomists say, assumes that we know God's nature or 'essence', and makes this the premise of a proof of God; he argues from essence to existence, whereas the only valid kind of argument to existence must start from existence (we argue, they claim, from the existence of the world to the existence of God). I shall discuss this so-called 'existentialist' approach in the next chapter; but I will say here yet again that the extent to which it is the essence or nature of God from which Anselm starts is minimal. A formal definition of the kind from which he begins is only in a marginal sense an account of the nature of God.

The upshot of the discussion so far will be clear enough. I do not think that the Ontological Argument, in the form in which it was presented by its originator, is as vulnerable to some of what may be called the standard criticisms as is generally thought. However, one important line of criticism of it—that it illegitimately treats existence as a property of things—I have not as yet mentioned; and another—the difficulties involved in the notion of necessary existence—I have mentioned but not discussed. It will be convenient to consider these in the context of Descartes's use of the argument and Kant's rejection of it.

Next to Anselm the best-known advocate of the Ontological Argument is René Descartes, philosopher and mathematician. Even more important as a critic of it than either Gaunilo or Aquinas is Kant, the greatest philosopher of the modern period.

Descartes, in his *Meditations*, seems to present the Ontological Argument as somewhat of an afterthought. He has already, in the Third Meditation, offered two arguments for God's existence (which will be discussed in the next chapter), and when in the Fifth Meditation he adds to these the Ontological Argument it may be with the intention less of clinching his proof of God than of bringing out clearly something about the God that he considers he has already sufficiently proved, namely, that God exists necessarily. On the other hand, there is a suggestion in the Fifth Meditation that the Ontological Argument is given as a demonstration of the existence of God; and in another of his works, the *Principles of Philosophy*, he seems clearly to be offering it as such. The ambiguity of his intentions in the *Meditations* has sometimes been accounted for as the effect of timidity. The Ontological Argument was looked on with disfavour by the Church at the time when Descartes wrote—in the eyes of the orthodox, Aquinas had decisively refuted it—and it has been suggested that he put out on display two arguments of an obviously acceptable character, and smuggled in the Ontological Argument later in the hope that it would not be noticed and that, if it were, its position as a lonely addition would make it easier to repudiate. That this interpretation is unflattering to Descartes is not of itself a reason for rejecting it. Still, this view of his motives is difficult to reconcile with the in fact rather prominent, because isolated, place, and quite lengthy presentation, that he gives to the Ontological Argument in the *Meditations*.

According to Descartes, the existence of God can be proved from a consideration of the perfections contained in the idea of God. The idea of God is the idea of an all-perfect being; and if God is all-perfect he must possess the perfection of existence. Existence is as much a part of the essence of God as in the case of a triangle it is part of its essence that the sum of its three angles is equal to 180 degrees. 'There is not any less repugnance to our conceiving a God (that is, a Being supremely perfect) to whom existence is lacking (that is to say, to whom a certain perfection is lacking) than to conceive of a mountain which has no valley' (Descartes, p. 181).

Descartes recognizes that from the fact that 'mountain' and 'valley' are correlative terms nothing follows about the existence of either mountains or valleys; for even if there were no mountains or valleys at all, except imaginary ones, it would still be the case that as we use the words it is impossible to conceive a mountain without a valley. (This is not strictly true, if we are to insist on the literal meanings of the words, for we can easily conceive of a mountain rising directly out of a plain: but Descartes's point is simply that we cannot conceive a mountain without neighbouring lower ground; it would not otherwise be a mountain.) But the case of God is different. It is not merely that, whether God exists or not, I cannot think of God without thinking of him as existing. It is not merely a matter of necessity in thought, as in the case of the triangle or that of the mountain; there is a necessity in things which itself determines my thought. An infinitely perfect being must possess the perfection of existence: I cannot conceive otherwise. Existence is inseparable from God; and therefore God really exists.

All this is reminiscent of Anselm—in its stress on the uniqueness of the idea of God, and on the notion of necessary existence—although Descartes makes no acknowledgement of indebtedness. But it is unlike what we found in Anselm in its claim to our possession of a clear and distinct idea of God (a marked feature of Descartes's argument; though I have not explicitly brought it out in my presentation) and in its explicit treatment of existence as a property—one 'perfection' among others possessed by the supremely perfect being.

Kant's attack on the Ontological Argument—it was he, incidentally, who first gave the argument that name—is directed more against Descartes's, or Leibniz's, version of it than against Anselm's. He treats it with some seriousness, on the ground that it is fundamental to the other theistic arguments, which do not stand on their own feet but travel a certain distance and then depend on the Ontological Argument to complete the journey. Thus, as Kant sees it, if it falls so, too, do the other theistic arguments.

Kant has a number of objections, but they reduce to two main lines of attack that can be summarized as follows. (6) From logical necessity to necessary existence: no road. (7) Existence is not a 'real' predicate. Let us look at each of these.

(6) The kind of necessity that belongs to propositions or statements (logical necessity) is not the same as the kind of necessity that is supposed to belong to God (necessary existence). To give examples of logical necessity is not to do anything that is of use

towards proving necessary existence; and the examples that are always given are examples of the former. Kant says that a typical argument would run like this: It is absolutely necessary that a triangle has three angles. This is indeed necessary; but note, it is logically necessary: the possession of three angles is necessary to being a triangle. The necessity lies in the proposition itself, 'A triangle has three angles', which is an analytic proposition. This does not say that three angles necessarily exist, but that, if a triangle exists, then it must necessarily have three angles. This kind of example could never be relevant to proving that a *Necessary Being* exists. If existence is made a defining characteristic of God then the proposition 'God exists' is indeed necessarily true, because analytic. But this only means that we have planted the idea of existence in the idea of God. We cannot go from this to the real necessary existence of God.

But, Kant holds, not only can we not pass from logical necessity to necessary existence; necessary existence is in any case a meaningless concept. Logical necessity is the only sort of necessity that we can conceive. We cannot think anything if we try to give content to the expression 'Being whose non-existence is inconceivable' or 'Being whose non-existence is impossible'. These are just empty sets of words: so God, as he is supposed to be understood in this Argument, is accordingly just an empty notion.

(7) Kant further holds that existence is not a 'real' predicate— which amounts to saying that it is not a real property of things. The existence of a thing is quite different from its colour, size, shape, etc. The latter are properties of the thing: its existence is not just an additional property. 'X is a, b, c, d, and it exists' says no more about the properties of X than does 'X is a, b, c, d'. Things exist with their properties, but existence itself is not an additional property.

One way—metaphorical, and liable to be somewhat misleading —of bringing out Kant's point about the difference between existence and properties is the following. It is as if there were two enormous boxes, one labelled 'Existents' and the other 'Non-entities'. Into the former box go, for instance, houses, with all their properties, and horses, with all theirs; into the latter, fairies and unicorns. Most people would put ghosts firmly into the second box; some would put them into the other; some may be in doubt. The question now is: Where do we put God? The Ontological Argument commits the absurdity of trying to guarantee that there is a place for God in the 'Existents' box by forcing the box itself into God. Existence just is not like this. It is much more like a receptacle into which we put some things and not others than it is like a feature possessed by some things and not by others. I would, however, caution the reader that this whole way of talking —'Existence is this or that, is not the other, etc.'—is, although completely natural, liable to mislead. 'Existence' is not the name of a thing, to be described in such terms, and the present paragraph must not be interpreted too literally.

Kant himself attempts to establish that existence is not a property by the following simple argument. If actual existence did add a property to a thing—something over and above what was conceived in the mere idea of it—then the existing thing could never be the same as what I had the idea of, but must be something different; and I could not say that what I conceived existed —it would always be something else (because something with an extra property that the mere conception could never have) that existed. (See Shaffer for a trenchant criticism of this Kantian argument, and in general for an illuminating discussion of the subject of this chapter.)

In saying that existence is not a real property Kant is surely right. In a sense, it does not matter greatly whether or not we call existence a property; but, if we do, we need to realize that at least it is a very different kind of property from the things that we generally call properties. However, it is not so certain that Kant is right in what he says about *necessary* existence: this we need to look at more closely. There are two separate, but closely related, questions here. First, whether although existence is not a property necessary existence may be; and, secondly, whether the concept of necessary existence is a meaningful one.

Professor Norman Malcolm has claimed that although existence is not a property necessary existence is. Now, Anselm, as we have noted more than once, says to God: 'Thou canst not be conceived not to be'. It is reasonable to interpret this as meaning that God, the being than which none greater can be conceived, possesses the property of not-being-able-to-be-conceived-as-not-existing. This does seem to be a perfectly genuine, if odd, property. If this is what necessary existence means (and I have yet to discuss fully what exactly Anselm means by it, or rather by his statement, 'Thou canst not be conceived not to be') then necessary existence is indeed a property.

Professor Malcolm himself argues from the view that necessary existence is a property to the validity of Anselm's Ontological Argument. Professor Malcolm's own argument here seems to depend on a particular interpretation of 'necessary existence'— to depend, in fact, on his understanding it in a sophisticated philosophical way as meaning something like 'existence whose denial would be self-contradictory'. I am extremely doubtful whether his interpretation expresses what Anselm in fact intended by his phrase, 'Thou canst not be conceived not to be' (cf. Hick). Professor Malcolm goes so far as to identify this philosophical notion of necessary existence with the notion contained in the opening words of Psalm xc: 'Before the mountains were brought forth, or ever thou hadst formed the earth and the world, even from everlasting to everlasting, thou art God' (Malcolm, p. 55). This is a plain misunderstanding of the quoted passage. There is not in the Hebrew anything corresponding to the philosophical notion of necessary existence: the meaning is perhaps that God outlasts the created world, that he existed before the creation of the world and will exist after the end of the world, but certainly not (what the philosopher would say) that it would be logically contradictory to deny his existence. But although 'from everlasting to everlasting' has nothing much to do with the philosophers' notion of necessary existence it does have, I think, a great deal to do with what Anselm meant by 'Thou canst not be conceived not to be'.

Let us turn for further illumination on this to the question whether the notion of necessary existence is meaningless. We have noted how central to Anselm's position is this notion. The definition that is his starting point does not explicitly refer to it, but before his Argument is over it has emerged as a vitally important part of the idea of God. To understand God fully is to understand him as necessarily existing; though the believer's initial understanding of God, like that of the atheist, may, of course, stop short of recognizing that necessary existence is involved in the notion of God as a being than which none greater can be conceived. What exactly did Anselm mean by the view of God as necessarily existing? He himself, of course, as I have indicated already, does not use the expression 'necessary existence'; and this is itself of some significance. It is people who expound Anselm's views or criticize them who say that he believed in the necessary existence of God. What he himself says is that God cannot be conceived as not existing, and by this he seems to mean the following three things at least. (a) He sometimes links it with the notion of degrees of existence—God exists more truly than other beings, other beings have less being than God. (b) He often links it with existence in time: for instance, in his Reply to Gaunilo he says that only things which have a beginning or end can be thought of as non-existent. (c) Also in the Reply he says that only beings which are composed of parts can be thought of as non-existent. The first and third of these are derived from Plato, and represent a point of view that I do not wish to defend. The second, which from the greater frequency of its occurrence we may suppose to be what Anselm himself wants to lay most weight on, is another matter. God is without beginning or end: this is what it chiefly means to say that he is a being than which none greater can be conceived. God does not come into existence; God does not pass out of existence.

'Whatever we conceive as existent, we can also conceive as non-existent. There is no being, therefore, whose non-existence implies a contradiction.' The quotation is not, as it happens, from Kant, but from David Hume (1711–76): the two philosophers are in entire agreement on this (Hume, Part IX, *ad fin.*). At first sight, Anselm may seem to be maintaining the exact opposite of this. But is he really denying what Hume asserts? Anselm does say that it is contradictory, supposing one grants that God is a being than which a greater cannot be conceived, to maintain at the same time that God might be thought of as not existing. This is not the same as saying that God is a being whose non-existence implies a contradiction. We have just seen the way in which Anselm himself explains what he means by

'Thou canst not be conceived not to be'. He does not mean that God's non-existence implies a contradiction. He means, for instance, that God has neither beginning nor end.

If Kant's and Hume's denial of meaning to the notion of necessary existence is to be effective towards refuting Anselm it must be taken as a denial of meaning to the notion that there is a being without beginning or end. Is such a notion meaningless? It certainly does not seem so. If the notion of necessary existence is indeed a meaningless one then it may be that Anselm's notion is not after all that of necessary existence. If, on the other hand, we allow that what Anselm is talking about is necessary existence then the Kantian dogma that the notion of necessary existence is meaningless needs re-examination.

I do not want to say that the Ontological Argument is valid as a proof of God. In maintaining that it is less vulnerable to criticism than has often been claimed I do not mean myself to claim that it is invulnerable to criticism. The blows can be softened: I do not think they can be entirely deflected.

It remains true that there is in this argument a movement from existence in the mind to existence in reality—or, better, from the concept of God to the existence of God—which, intuitively, one is impelled to resist, though the assigning of precise grounds for rejecting it is not, as I hope I have shown, as simple a matter as is often supposed. The instinct of Thomists like Professor Mascall in rejecting the *a priori* approach of Anselm's Ontological Argument in favour of the *a posteriori* approach seen in their version of the Cosmological Argument is a sound one; even though, as I have suggested earlier, Thomists do not always by any means do Anselm justice and tend, it seems to me, to exaggerate the differences between him and their own master.

The value of the Ontological Argument—at least in its Anselmian version—is great. It lies in the Anselmian combination of rationality with faith, no less than in the way it brings to the forefront the notion of the necessary existence of God and raises the question of how this notion is to be understood. This Argument, and the Cosmological Argument to which we are about to turn, raise issues utterly fundamental to a philosophical study of religion, and in particular to a study of the place of reason in religion.

Let us return finally to the point that was developed in the earlier part of the chapter. It is not as a 'proof' of God—something that might convince an unbeliever—that the so-called Ontological Argument deserves to be taken seriously. From that point of view it is a failure, even when considered in its subtle Anselmian form. Its chief value, I should claim, lies rather in the contribution that it, together with the other 'proofs' of God, can make to the clarification of the concept of God itself and of what is meant by belief in God. It is only, I should further claim, by the examination *in detail* of the Ontological Argument and its fellow theistic 'proofs' that we can see their contribution to this clarification.

CHAPTER 5

From Effect to Cause

IN SHARP contrast to the Ontological Argument are those arguments that we are now to consider. These are arguments for God that consist fundamentally in arguing from Creation to Creator: from the world considered as effect, to God as its only possible cause. 'If anything exists, God exists': so this line of argument has been summed up. We ourselves, and all about us, are *dependent*; and from the mere existence of ourselves, or of anything else, we are led to God as, ultimately, the only adequate cause on which we and they depend. The most famous argument of this kind is the Cosmological Argument; and the most famous version of the Cosmological Argument is that of St. Thomas Aquinas. In addition to Aquinas's, I shall also consider in the present chapter arguments of Descartes and of Bishop Berkeley.

It is an *interpretation* of Aquinas that I shall be presenting in what follows. It is the most usual interpretation, but nevertheless it is a matter open to dispute whether this is what Aquinas actually meant. To forestall possible criticism I had better say at the outset that whether or not Aquinas really meant what I say he meant is irrelevant to my purpose in this chapter. I am setting out to discuss a certain view or set of views, and it is largely a matter of indifference whose names are attached to them. In this particular instance, much more than in most, to enter into controversy about how authors ought to be interpreted, though certainly of importance, would not markedly assist our enterprise. What I am writing about in this chapter is *causal* arguments to the existence of God. The Cosmological Argument has commonly been represented as a causal argument, but there are certainly those who would deny that it is this. I shall merely state that this is how I propose to take it.

We have already seen that Aquinas rejected Anselm's Ontological Argument. It seemed to him that from the mere idea of God we cannot argue to God's existence. Only from existence can we validly argue to existence. In following out this line of thought Aquinas used, though he did not originate, the complex of proofs known as the Five Ways, which in their most distinctive aspect constitute his version of the Cosmological Argument.

Thomas Aquinas was born near Naples in 1224 or 1225, of noble family. He became a Dominican friar in 1244, against the wishes of his family: not that they had any objection to the Church, but they had ecclesiastical ambitions for Thomas of an altogether grander kind than anything they thought his life with the Dominicans was likely to lead to. He was kidnapped by his brothers, but was true to his Order in spite even of the temptations of Saint Anthony to which his relatives hopefully exposed him. He went to Paris; and there, and later in Cologne, he learnt a great deal from Albert the Great, who in his turn showed particular interest in this most promising pupil. Thomas became professor in Paris, then at the Papal Court, then in Paris again, and finally in Naples. In 1274 he set off for Lyons, whither he had been summoned to the Council by Pope Gregory X; he was taken ill on the way and died peacefully, after a comparatively brief life (he was forty-nine) at a Cistercian monastery near the beaches of Anzio.

One of the most likeable of men, and one of the greatest of thinkers, Aquinas, whose writings were voluminous, has attained something of the status of official philosopher to the Roman Catholic Church. He combined the attitude of the philosopher with that of the devout believer in God, and at no time wished to exalt reason over faith: near the end of his life he remarked, 'All that I have written seems to me like so much straw compared with what I have seen and with what has been revealed to me'. But his attitude was not the same as Anselm's. He did not insist that belief must precede understanding. On the contrary, it seemed to him important that the existence of God should be accepted as a matter capable of conclusive demonstration and not dependent on initial faith. There was plenty of room for faith; but in his endeavour to develop a systematic theology Aquinas adopted the method of first proving what could be proved, or what he thought could be proved, in the hope of thus providing a firm foundation on which the superstructure of faith could be built.

In carrying out this programme he took over some of the methods and ideas of Aristotle. By Aquinas's day, the name of Aristotle had come to stand for *the* Philosopher, though to some his philosophy appeared hardly compatible with the Christian faith. In his greatest work, the *Summa Theologica*, as elsewhere, Aquinas set himself to present Christianity to his fellow-theologians in Aristotelian terms—or, more strictly, in terms drawn from both Augustine and Aristotle. He was himself genuinely fired with enthusiasm for Aristotle's philosophy, and it did not seem to him—and in this he was developing the view of his master St. Albert—that there was any conflict between this pagan philosophy and Christianity; he thought, indeed, that nothing but good could come from a merger between them.

The Five Ways of St. Thomas Aquinas are taken largely from Aristotle, and can be put as follows.

1. *Argument from Motion or Change*. We know that some things move. The sense of 'move' here is that of movement from potentiality to actuality: what a thing is only potentially it is made actually; as wood which is potentially hot is made actually hot by fire. Now each thing that moves must be moved by some other thing (wood does not make itself hot), and if that moves it must in its turn be moved by something else again, and *that* by yet another thing, and so on. There cannot be an infinite regress of movers, because then the process would not be complete and nothing could ever move at all. So there must be a *first* mover—an unmoved mover—to start the whole process off. This first mover all men understand to be God.

2. *Argument to a First Cause*. The Second Way is parallel to the First; though whereas there Aquinas considered things as acted upon, here he considers them rather as agents. We find among phenomena an order of efficient causality. Now, nothing can be the efficient cause of itself; to be that it would have to be prior to itself, which is impossible. So each thing that is caused must be caused by some other thing, and that by something else again,

and *that* by yet another thing, and so on. There cannot, in an ordered series, be an infinite regress of causes, because then the process would not be complete and nothing could ever have been caused at all. So there must be a *first* efficient cause—an uncaused cause—to start the whole process off. This first cause all men understand to be God.

3. *Argument from Possibility and Necessity.* We find that there are things that are possible to be or not to be; for they come into existence and pass away again. These may be said to exist contingently. (Aquinas himself does not use the word 'contingent', and it is only fair to say that not all his modern followers would be content to see this word used in expounding him.) Now it is impossible that *everything* that exists has only this kind of existence; for if that were so there must have once been a time when nothing existed at all: but at that time there would be no reason why anything should begin to be (for that which does not exist can only begin to exist through something that already exists), and accordingly nothing would ever have come to exist. Obviously, things do exist here and now. It follows that not everything that exists exists contingently; there must be a necessary being. This being all men understand to be God.

4. *Argument from Degrees of Perfection.* Some things are said to be better than others. To say that one thing is better than another can only mean that it approaches more nearly to the best or perfect. A perfect being therefore exists. And the perfect being is the *cause* of all other beings (as the maximum of a genus is the cause of all in that genus; for instance, fire is the cause of all hot things). We understand this perfect being to be God.

5. *Teleological Argument.* There is evidence of purpose or intention in the behaviour of inanimate or unreflecting things. So there must be a supreme intelligence behind the universe that directs natural things towards ends, 'as the arrow is directed by the archer'. This supreme intelligence we call God.

So much for a statement of the Five Ways. It will be seen that, taken together, with the possible exception of the Fifth Way, they aim at showing that there is a necessary being, who (or which) is the cause of the world. It has been claimed that Aquinas did himself intend that they should always be taken together. On this view, the Five Ways are not to be regarded as five separate arguments. None of them is intended, alone, as a proof of God. Taken alone they would prove, if anything, only, respectively, a first mover, a first cause, a necessary being, a perfect being, and an intelligent being. There seems to be no particular reason to suppose that Aquinas did in fact want the Five Ways to be regarded at all times as a group. Nevertheless, there is some value in the suggestion that they all hang together, and that you cannot prove God unless you use them all. Of course, even when they are taken together Aquinas does not suppose that they prove the Christian God. Like Anselm, he finds it essential to follow up the statement of the argument for God's existence with a discussion of the attributes of God. God, in the full Christian meaning of the word, cannot be proved by argument; but the rather abstract and impersonal being that can, Aquinas thinks, be proved, is at least a foundation for a full Christian belief.

In discussing the Five Ways, we are bound to begin, I think, by considering them singly. I do not deny that perhaps a complex of arguments may sometimes prove more than do the parts of that complex considered as separate units: but we need to set against this the proverbial fact that weakness in its links makes for weakness in a chain. I shall accordingly look at each of the Ways in turn before coming on to discuss the question of their underlying unity.

1 and 2. A difficulty that has often been felt here is that of deciding what exactly is meant by the notion of a 'First' Cause and a 'First' Mover. If what is meant is merely—so to speak— the first in the line of ordinary causes or movers, then the First Cause or First Mover is only a cause or mover like the others, and it is hard to see why such a cause or mover should be given the special status of Uncaused Cause or Unmoved Mover. If, on the other hand, the First Cause or the First Mover stands right outside the line of ordinary causes and movers, it must be so different from other causes and movers that it is hard to see in what sense it can be called a cause or a mover at all. In other words, we understand the notion of cause or mover as applied to contingent things, and it is unclear what it means as it is used in the Cosmological Argument; that is, as applied to the relation between a necessary being and contingent things. (This is, of

course, only one instance of the general problem of what, when they are applied to God, is meant by words whose normal meaning is tied to things of more ordinary experience—a problem that Aquinas himself attempts to solve in his Doctrine of Analogy. I shall have something to say about analogy in Chapter 12.) It has been claimed that the notion of causality of which Aquinas is making use—it has been called 'metaphysical causality' (see Mascall (2), p. 75 fn.)—is uncongenial to the modern scientific mind, so that this whole way of arguing, which may have seemed to make good sense in the thirteenth century, makes no sense now. The notion of 'metaphysical causality' is certainly one to which it is difficult to attach meaning. Professor Mascall, in introducing the term, refers to 'a confusion between metaphysical causality and the purely descriptive causality of the physical sciences'. But the term 'metaphysical causality' may well be itself the result of a confusion between 'cause' and 'explanation' (perhaps deriving from Aristotle's so-called four causes, which are in reality four kinds of explanation). It is not at all easy to see what might be meant by 'metaphysical *causality*', and this is not simply a matter of its uncongeniality to the modern scientific mind. Simply to replace it by the expression 'metaphysical explanation' would not fit the Thomists' bill; for then we should have departed from the notion of a First *Cause* or First *Mover*.

A difficulty is sometimes raised over the notion of an infinite regress. It is said that we can refuse to accept Aquinas's apparent assumption that unless the series of causes or movers has a beginning nothing could ever have come to be. Why should there not be an infinite regress of causes or movers? There is no contradiction involved in supposing this.

Against this it is often claimed nowadays by Thomists that Aquinas's point is not so much that an infinite regress is impossible as that it gets us no nearer the solution of the problem. To account for individual members of a chain of cause or motion in terms of earlier ones *even to infinity* would not ultimately explain why anything is as it is here and now: the more items we bring into the account the more we merely multiply our problem; for the earlier items themselves need accounting for just as much as the later. The problem is one of conservation more than creation.

E

'The real lesson which the First Way forces upon us [is that] the first mover must itself be motionless not merely in such a way as to provide the sequence of *moventia* and *mota* with a first term, but in such a way as to maintain the motion which is a feature of the sequence as a whole' (Mascall (2), p. 74). 'Aquinas is not rejecting the possibility of an infinite series as such . . . . He does not mean to rule out the possibility of an infinite series of causes and effects, in which a given member depended on the preceding member, say *X* on *Y*, but does not, once it exists, depend here and now on the present causal activity of the preceding member. We have to imagine, not a lineal or horizontal series, so to speak, but a vertical hierarchy, in which a lower member depends here and now on the present causal activity of the member above it. It is the latter type of series, if prolonged to infinity, which Aquinas rejects' (Copleston, p. 118).

It is not easy to see how interpretations of this kind answer the original objection. Whether there is a 'vertical' series of causes, as here defined, is really the point at issue (and vertical causality is, anyway, as odd a notion as metaphysical causality). Certainly, if we are to suppose a series of causes or of movement such that each item requires for its existence the continuing activity *here and now* of the items above it in the series, we *may* be led to admit a First Cause; though even here we might resist a little longer. But the question really is whether there *is* a causal series of this 'vertical' type; whether, in fact, an account of causality in terms of 'lineal' or 'horizontal' series (which Thomists admit might well be infinite) is not perfectly adequate. We are back, in fact, at Professor Mascall's contrast between 'the purely descriptive causality of the physical sciences' and 'metaphysical' causality. To accept metaphysical causality is indeed to be well on the way to theism. But that there is such a thing as metaphysical causality is not self-evident; and the determined non-theist will have no difficulty in not accepting it. We see once again that 'proof' of God is not to be divorced from prior belief in God; as Anselm saw so clearly, and as Aquinas (as far as his procedure in the Five Ways is concerned, though not more generally) tries not to see.

3. The same contrast inspires our comment on the Third Way. It is *not* impossible that everything that exists may exist only

contingently. Admittedly, there was then a time when any given thing did not exist, but this does not entitle us to say that there was a time when nothing at all existed. Aquinas did not deny the possibility of a beginningless universe. The coming into being and passing away of things may have always overlapped, so that there was never a time when nothing at all existed. One contingent thing causes another, and there is no need to bring in a necessary being at all—unless, of course, with the Thomists referred to, one insists on taking the view of the so-called vertical as opposed to the horizontal series.

4. It does not follow from the fact that we judge one thing better than another that there must exist a best. One thing's being better than another is relative, and does not necessarily imply the actual existence of the ideal, the best, the perfect. Take a specific case. Some things are hotter than others. But they are so simply by contrast with neighbouring things that are comparatively less hot. We do not need to postulate an absolutely hottest thing in order to make sense of our talk about degrees of heat. In any case, the notion of an absolutely hottest thing is doubtfully meaningful, as we saw in our discussion in the previous chapter of attributes without intrinsic maxima. No more, then, need we postulate an unqualified best or perfect being in order to make sense of our use of comparatives in general.

You could, of course, say that we have the *idea* of a best or perfect being by which we judge all others. But you cannot get from this mere idea to the actual existence of such a being. To think you could would be to think that the Ontological Argument was valid; and Aquinas himself, of course, rejects the Ontological Argument.

The notion that the Supremely Good Being is the *cause* of being in other things—a notion which derives ultimately from Plato—is, again, far from self-evident.

5. The Teleological Argument, or Argument from Design, is to be discussed fully in the next chapter, so nothing further need be said about it here.

We have considered the Five Ways separately. Let us now consider them together. If we try to take the Five Ways as a single, if complex, argument, and look for the underlying unity behind the apparent diversity, what do we find? From one point of view, I have answered this question already. The Five Ways, taken together, are directed at showing that there is a necessary being who is the cause of the world. What we must now do is look somewhat more closely into the implications of this statement.

The notion of cause is presented not merely in the Second Way; it is also contained in the others, in the sense that the common conclusion of the Five Ways is clearly intended to be that the cosmos is an *effect* (or, more generally, is *dependent*), and hence suggests a *cause*. The notion of necessary existence belongs explicitly in the Third Way; but, as Thomists tend to interpret the Five Ways, its presence is also, though not perhaps so obviously, to be detected throughout. In particular, it is often suggested, the first three of the Five Ways ought to be considered as in a very real sense a single argument; the First and Second being strictly preliminary to the Third, and not to be understood except in the light of it. This view has already been referred to. God is not *first* cause or mover in the sense of standing at the beginning of a temporal series of causes or movement—whether as himself the first item in the series or even simply as a force exerted from outside upon the series in order to get it going. God is first in the sense of most important: 'first' as opposed to 'secondary'; not 'first' as opposed to 'later'. God is the necessary being metaphorically standing above (or below) all contingent things in a wholly timeless sense, and upholding by his mysterious power all motion and all causal connexions. Sometimes this relation between Creator and Creation—'the cosmological relation', as Dr. Austin Farrer has called it—would be said to be not strictly a causal relation at all, but a unique relation which can be described in the language of cause and effect only by analogy.

These are ways in which some modern Thomists would present the Cosmological Argument. Whether such versions of it do, as tends to be claimed, no more than bring out what Aquinas himself intended, or whether, on the other hand, they go beyond the Five Ways, does not concern us. The views of present-day Thomists are worth examining for their own sakes. It may, however, be proper to say that Aquinas himself, if we are to judge by his general attitude, would have wished nothing better than that subsequent thinkers should re-interpret and improve on the Five Ways. He did not aim to produce a final, canonized philosophy; though some of his more pedestrian followers have sometimes behaved as if he had in fact done so.

The sort of view that I have in mind can be expressed as follows; it is difficult to put it otherwise than rather loosely. What is being argued is that if we look about us at the world in which we live, or if, for that matter, we look within ourselves, what will strike us is the finiteness of things. As Professor Mascall puts it, what strikes us is that things are 'not able to account for their own existence' (Mascall (2), Chap. IV, *passim*). Reflection on the finiteness of things (or, to change the terminology, on the contingency of things) leads us inexorably to an Infinite Being (or, a Necessary Being) without which the finite (or contingent) could not exist at all. It is as simple as that. There is no need to bother overmuch, we may suppose, with the complications of St. Thomas's own quinquefarious presentation.

This, then, it is claimed, is the fundamental idea behind the Cosmological Argument. What is involved is, as the point is sometimes put, a 'cosmological insight'—a certain way of seeing things. The Cosmological Argument, indeed, it is sometimes said, is not exactly an argument at all; for to call it that suggests something too formal, too strict. We see that there must be a God; and we see this in a way that it is not easy to reduce to the straitjacket of an argument. We grasp that God exists, we see him 'in the cosmological relation', or in the relation of infinite to finite; and this we do by attending to the character of the world in which we live—its character of, to quote the phrase again, not being able to account for its own existence.

There are three comments that I should like to make on this modern version of the Cosmological Argument.

(1) I have already remarked that as so presented it is not an argument in any very strict or 'formal' sense. This is in any case recognized by modern Thomists themselves; and to call attention to it need not of itself imply criticism. After all, it might be said that any presentation of the so-called proofs of the existence of

God as something less than strict arguments is, in view of the extent to which they have been criticized, only an open and honest facing of facts. I think there is nevertheless sometimes a certain conflict in the Thomist position—a conflict connected with this admission that the Cosmological Argument is perhaps not really an argument. Thomists, as part of their criticism of the Ontological Argument, tend to make the point that we do not immediately 'see' God as he is in himself; we apprehend him only in the cosmological relation, as the phrase I quoted earlier has it. We do not, in other words, have 'direct', 'immediate' knowledge of God. This seems to mean that an element of inference, of some kind or other, must come into our knowledge of him. If this is so, the Cosmological Argument, in the version that I am considering, might be said both to be and not to be an argument. It is not a strict argument, as we have agreed; and it is probably all the better for that. But nor, on Thomist principles, is it merely a misleading way of saying that some people just 'see' that there is a God without having to go through a process of inference of any kind.

We cannot take too literally the notion that something might both be and not be an argument. In particular, there is a difference between being an argument, however loose and informal, and being a statement of the obvious. Consider the following: 'If we come to see the finiteness of the world we shall see that there must be a God'. What is the logical status of this statement? From one point of view it might be taken as expressing an inference: from another it might be taken as simply a truism. It is an inference if seeing the finiteness of the world is taken to mean seeing some feature of the world *other than* seeing God in—or, better, 'beyond'—it. But it is simply a truism, and no argument, if seeing the finiteness of the world is taken to mean seeing the world in the way that Thomists tend to suggest that they see it; that is, seeing it as having the sort of existence that only makes sense when understood in contrast to the sort of existence God has.

To explain this latter point more fully. 'Finite' is a word with various meanings, but however it is used it must always be understood in relation to a corresponding sense of 'infinite'. Now 'finite', as the Thomist uses it, is naturally understood by contrast with 'infinite' as this latter term is applied to God. To say the world is finite is to say that it is limited, *as God is unlimited*, that it cannot account for its own existence, *as God can account for his*, etc. Thus, from the Thomist point of view, to say 'The world is finite'—*really meaning what you say*—may be precisely to say 'There is an Infinite Being'; for otherwise—still from the Thomist point of view—'The world is finite' makes no sense. To return to the previous way of putting it, the Thomist, in saying, 'If we come to see the finiteness of the world we shall see that there must be a God', may be saying, 'If we come to see that the world cannot account for its own existence but must be accounted for as the work of a Divine Creator, we shall see that the world must be accounted for as the work of a Divine Creator'. This is indubitably true; but it is hardly informative: it is, as I say, simply a truism.

(2) Suppose now we do take this version of the Cosmological Argument *as* an argument, and leave aside the particular difficulty that I have just been discussing. It seems to me that the argument is at fault in that it misplaces the inferential step. What is suggested is that the world exhibits a positive feature called the feature of being finite. This is something that the reflective man is supposed to recognize, though not, it may be, altogether without difficulty. Having recognized it, he has then to be persuaded to take the step of inferring from this to an Infinite Being as the necessary ground of the finite world. This does not ring true. The inferential step does not come here; it must come earlier. What the reflective man is likely to need most persuasion about is the finiteness of the world, in the sense that the Thomist understands this. Such persuasion is just what Aquinas himself was offering in the Five Ways; and the modern Thomist may well lose more than he gains by searching too exclusively for unity behind Aquinas's variety. When he has come to see this he does not need further persuasion to recognize an Infinite Being; he has recognized this Being already. What is difficult is to get people to acknowledge in the first place that the world 'cannot account for its own existence'. There is no difficulty in getting people who have acknowledged this to acknowledge a Creator; for that acknowledgement is implicit in the other. In so far as the Cosmo-

logical Argument is sometimes presented as if it rested on an obvious and indubitable feature of the world—its finiteness, in the particular sense of the Thomists—it is misleading. The point at issue between Christian and sceptic may be said to be precisely this: whether or not the world *is* 'finite'. In order that a man who does not see this may come to see it he needs to make a change in his outlook of a very fundamental kind.

Indeed, it is true to say, I think, that the value of the Cosmological Argument lies not in any efficacy it may have as a proof of God, but in its bringing out so sharply the fact that the Christian believer, on one definition of him, anyway, is the man who 'sees the world to be finite', or 'sees the things of the world to be incapable of accounting for their own existence'.

(3) I have mentioned in the previous chapter the fact that modern Thomists sometimes claim that their position is 'existentialist' (in the sense that they want to argue to the existence of God from that of the world) as opposed to Anselm's, which they would describe as 'essentialist' (in the sense that he argues to the existence of God from the essence of God). It is worth noting that one implication of the foregoing is that the Thomist 'existentialist' position is not as purely existentialist as some Thomists would like to think. Those Thomists who would say that they are arguing from the finiteness of the world must answer the charge that they are arguing from the world as having a certain character; which is to say that they are arguing from the essence of the world. Such Thomists are not arguing from the mere existence of the world; they are arguing from the fact, as they see it, that it is not able to account for its own existence. Equally, of course, as 'finite' and 'infinite' are correlative terms, they are not arguing *to* the mere existence of God; they are arguing to a God who is, presumably, 'able to account for his own existence', and this is something about the essence of God. Essence and existence are not, in fact, to be separated; as Thomists in their better moments recognize.

The Five Ways and modern explications of them are not the only kind of causal argument to the existence of God. I shall now examine the two arguments which were presented by Descartes in his Third Meditation. These occupy a particular context in Descartes's philosophy. Descartes, a rationalist (in the usual philosophical sense, where rationalism is opposed to empiricism), is seeking sure and certain knowledge. His senses he distrusts because they sometimes deceive him. His method is to try to doubt everything that can possibly be doubted, in the hope of finding that there is something that cannot be doubted, something that can be used as the starting point of sure and certain knowledge. He finds this indubitable something in the very fact of his doubting. Whatever else can be doubted, one thing at least cannot: that Descartes is doubting. To doubt is to think. So it is utterly certain that Descartes is thinking. If he is thinking he must exist. 'I think, therefore I am' (*Cogito, ergo sum*). 'But what then am I?' Descartes's answer is: 'A thing which thinks. What is a thing which thinks? It is a thing which doubts, understands, [conceives], affirms, denies, wills, refuses, which also imagines and feels' (Descartes, p. 153). This is the point from which he goes on to recover, but now (he considers) on a sure and certain foundation, everything about which he had previously had doubts. An early step in this process is to prove the existence of God.

Descartes's arguments may be put (roughly) as follows.

1. I have the idea of God in my mind. This is an idea which I could never have thought of for myself. Only God could have put it in my mind. Therefore God exists.

2. I exist. My existence must be dependent on some author, i.e. something must have caused me to exist. This something can only be God. Therefore God exists.

These, it is clear, are causal arguments. Descartes is arguing, first, from the actual idea of God in his, Descartes's mind, and, second, from himself, Descartes; in each case, to God as the only possible cause of these things. As we noted in the previous chapter, Descartes does not make use of the Ontological Argument until a later stage of the *Meditations*; after, in fact, he has (as he sees it) satisfactorily proved God. His first argument is not unlike the Ontological Argument to the extent that both make use of the idea of God. There is nevertheless a world of difference between them. Descartes is here arguing primarily from the existence of this idea in his mind, and only secondarily from its content. Let us now look in detail at Descartes's two causal arguments.

1. What Descartes is saying amounts to this. I have the idea of God. I could not have this idea unless there were a God; for the idea of God is the idea of an Infinite Being, and I, as a finite being, could never have thought of this idea by myself. I could only have it if an Infinite Being had implanted it in my mind; therefore an Infinite Being exists; i.e., God exists. My idea of an Infinite Being is, then, caused by, or is the effect of, a real Infinite Being.

Descartes himself now considers objections that might be brought against his argument, and attempts to answer them. These objections and answers provide an essential clarification of the argument. There are three objections.

It might be said, in the first place, that I arrive at the idea of an Infinite Being merely by negating my idea of finite being; and that there is therefore no need to invoke a real Infinite Being to implant the idea in me. Descartes answers that the notion of the infinite is 'more real' than that of the finite and is therefore 'in some way' prior to that of the finite. I could not know myself to be finite except by comparison with my idea of the infinite.

It might be said, secondly, that the idea of an Infinite Being is just an illusion anyway. Descartes answers that it cannot be, because (a) it is very clear and distinct, and (b) it contains more objective reality than any other. (*Objective* reality, in Descartes's terminology, is the kind of reality that ideas have, in so far as they are 'representations' of objects; *formal* reality is basically the kind of reality that real objects themselves have. This is a somewhat confusing terminology. As Descartes uses the expressions 'objective reality' and 'formal reality', they mean the opposite of what we would be inclined to expect them to mean.)

Finally, it might be said that I get the idea of an Infinite Being merely by extending my own qualities. Perhaps the perfections that I attribute to God are really present in myself, though only potentially. In particular, I can easily imagine my knowledge being perfected, and I can imagine myself in consequence acquiring the other perfections that I think of as divine. What need then for a cause other than myself for my idea of God? Descartes answers that this cannot be so, because (a) my knowledge is only potential, whereas my idea of the deity is of a being with its perfections actually existent (it is, indeed, a mark of *im*perfection in knowledge that it may be augmented); and (b) my knowledge can never be infinite—it will never reach perfection, will never cease to improve—whereas I conceive God as actually infinite.

These objections and answers make it quite clear that Descartes's first argument is based on specific Cartesian axioms: and only if these are accepted—only, one might say, if the whole Cartesian approach to philosophy is adopted—will his arguments seem cogent. It is an axiom for Descartes that an idea that is very clear and distinct must be true. It is equally an axiom for him that there are degrees of reality, and that ideas with a high degree of objective reality must be caused by things with a high degree of formal reality. If you do not think that clarity and distinctness in an idea are marks of truth (or if you do not in any case think that the idea of God is clear and distinct), and if you do not think that there are degrees of reality, you will not find Descartes's first argument cogent. The latter axiom I shall refer to again below; the former I shall comment on now.

On this question of clarity and distinctness Descartes the Rationalist is, in a sense, not being enough of a rationalist. On the face of it, it would seem more 'rational' to suppose that any idea that finite (weak, limited) human minds might hold of the infinite or transcendent will be bound to be *un*clear and *in*distinct. Descartes admits that the finite cannot comprehend the infinite, but he holds that nevertheless, as far as it goes, we have a clear and distinct idea of God—that is, he means, the idea of God is clearly present to the mind and is precisely distinguished from other ideas. Descartes needs to maintain the truth of 'God exists'. God is necessary to him as an element in the process of building up sure and certain knowledge (God exists, he argues, and is not a deceiver, so he would not permit me to be deceived in every-thing I think I know, etc.). But, on his principles, to maintain the truth of 'God exists' involves maintaining that the idea of God is clear and distinct. This is flying in the face of common sense, and an instance of how Rationalists in philosophy can be too

rational, in the sense of too much concerned with consistency and
system; and consequently, as I have just remarked, not rational
enough, in the sense of not sufficiently concerned with what is
commonsensical, to be expected, etc. Certainly, if the general
criterion of truth is clarity and distinctness, then either belief in
God must be clear and distinct or it must be false. But if we start
from the position, *prima facie* at least as reasonable as this, that
some true beliefs are clear and distinct and others are unclear
and indistinct, the situation becomes very different. On the other
hand, Descartes does have a point here. If a belief were really
very unclear and indistinct, in his sense of these words, how could
we know for sure what it is a belief in, and how therefore could
we know whether it is true or false?

2. Let us now pass to Descartes's second argument. This can
conveniently be re-expressed in a series of stages.

(1) Either I am caused or I am not caused. But I cannot be
not caused; for I am undoubtedly conserved, and conservation
is one aspect of causation. So I am caused.

(2) There must be as much reality in a cause as in its effect
(Cartesian axiom). I am a thinking thing, so my cause must be
a thinking thing.

Therefore: (3) I am caused by something which is (*a*) capable
of conserving me, and (*b*) a thinking thing, and (*c*) as we learned
from the previous proof, capable of implanting in me the idea of
an absolutely perfect being.

(4) My cause may be:

(i) Myself. But: (*a*) I have no power of conserving myself; (*b*)
if I were my own cause I should know myself to be God, but as I
know myself to be imperfect I cannot be God.

(ii) My parents. But: (*a*) they have no power to conserve me;
(*b*) they caused my body, but not me as a thinking thing; (*c*)
they have not the perfections that I have an idea of.

(iii) A number of co-operating causes. But: my idea of God
contains the idea of unity as one of his perfections; the idea of
God is the idea of *one* being possessing all the other perfections.

(iv) God. Only God is (*a*) capable of conserving me; and (*b*)
a thinking thing; and (*c*) has the perfections that I have an idea of.

Therefore: my cause is God.

(5) That is, God exists.

In commenting on this argument I shall go through in order the points that I have distinguished.

(1) Descartes is right to insist on the importance of conservation. The modern interpretation of the Five Ways that we considered above does the same. The upholding of the world is at least as important a part of religious belief as is its creation.

But, although connected, these things are not identical. To prove conservation would not necessarily be to prove creation, and *vice versa*; though to prove conservation might well be enough to prove *God*.

The use of 'cause' here is odd. We do not often say 'cause to exist'; we say rather 'cause to fall', etc. The natural word to use if you mean 'cause to exist' is 'create'. But if by 'cause' Descartes means 'create' (as, of course, he does: and, in any case, he also uses 'create' itself) he is begging the question. That I or anything else is *created* assumes God; for God is precisely the being that does create. Uses of the word in other contexts—artistic 'creation', for instance—are clearly analogical. There is only sense, analogical occasions apart, in talking of something or somebody being created if you mean that *God* did it. The case is the same with 'conserve'. 'I am conserved' begs the question; for what but God can conserve, in the sense intended? Just continuing to be requires no effort on a person's part: but 'conserve' does contain the idea of an effort—as if I might suddenly slip out of existence if somebody were not constantly watching over me to ensure that I did not literally become a nonentity. It would be absurd to suggest that I or any other human being could perform this function, except in medical or allied senses which are not in question here. Only God could do this; and in putting the matter in terms of conservation (= cause = putting forth of power) Descartes is inserting his answer into his question.

(2) Here we return to the Cartesian axiom about degrees of reality, and about the necessity for things with objective reality (ideas) to be caused by things with formal reality. Terminology apart, I do not wish to quarrel with this. We may agree with Descartes that a non-existent thing could not cause something to exist (i.e. create it), nor could something with only objective

reality create or conserve something with formal reality. Of course, ideas do sometimes cause things. Ideas have caused revolutions. But this kind of causation is hardly *creation* as Descartes is here considering it. And, in any case, although ideas may 'cause' things, people cause the ideas in the first place. Marxism may have caused new social structures; but it took Marx to cause Marxism.

(3) and (4) The 'I' that is caused is 'a thinking thing'. In the phrase coined by Professor Gilbert Ryle to characterize Descartes's view, it is 'the Ghost in the Machine' (Ryle, pp. 15–16). This is of considerable importance for Descartes's theistic arguments, and we need to pause for a moment on this point.

Descartes was much influenced by the sudden development of natural science that took place about and just before his time. He is himself an important figure in the history of mathematics as well as of philosophy; he was the founder of analytic or co-ordinate geometry. Descartes's interest in physics led him to take a mechanistic view of things. He thought, even, that animals are just machines. And so is the human body; though the human being is more than his body. Indeed, the other part of the human being—the mind, or the 'Ghost' in Professor Ryle's phrase—is a much more important part than the body. The trouble about machines is that they do not last for ever. They break down; they rust and decay. Animals die; human bodies die, too. Descartes was much interested in the question of immortality. He says in the Dedication of the *Meditations*: 'I have always been of the opinion that the two questions respecting God and the soul were the chief of those that ought to be determined by the help of philosophy rather than by that of theology'. His central questions are those of the immortality of the soul and the existence of God. His solution of both these problems depends on the distinction of body and mind. It has often been remarked that in drawing this distinction as sharply as he does, Descartes gave to modern philosophy its central problem; the problem of fitting together again what he had divided.

Clearly, if everything in the universe is simply mechanical then there is no sense in talking of immortality. If there is to be anything in the universe that is immortal it must be non-mechanical.

So Descartes made his division of mind from body. Bodies are mechanical and come to an end. The soul is not mechanical; never breaks down or wears out or rusts, but goes on for ever.

By bodies Descartes means physical bodies—like stones, lumps of lead, the stars and planets; and animals and human bodies. Body, says Descartes, is divisible, corporeal substance, which produces heat and movement. A living body is 'a machine made by the hands of God, which is incomparably better arranged and adequate to movements more admirable than is any machine of human invention'. The soul, or mind, is indivisible, thinking substance. It is the agency which understands, thinks, wills, imagines and remembers. The understanding, the will, the imagination and the memory are not *parts* of the mind; the mind is indivisible; it is the same mind which thinks, wills, imagines, and remembers. And mind is not a part of the soul, as his predecessors said; it is another name for it. For 'soul' Descartes substitutes indifferently 'mind', 'spirit', 'reason', 'understanding', 'intellect', 'intelligence', or 'a thinking thing'.

The distinction between body and soul is fundamental to Descartes's philosophy; though that is not to say that he explicitly starts by drawing the distinction. It is truer to say that he was driven to it. However he got to it, if he had not drawn this distinction, he might never have needed to prove God's existence. The famous *Cogito* argument, as we have noted, is not taken by him to be a proof that he, Descartes, exists as a body plus a mind; he takes it as proving only that he exists as 'a thinking thing'. His body has yet to be proved; and the proof of God, to which he proceeds, is necessary in order that his body and his sense experience should be placed upon a rational foundation. If he had not adopted the body/mind distinction, Descartes might very well not have felt the need for God as an element in his philosophical system; and if he had nevertheless, for some other reason, wanted to prove God, it is certain that he would not have felt bound to present his proofs precisely in the way he did. The form of his second argument is determined by the assumption that what is meant by 'I' is not 'a body plus a mind' but 'a thinking thing' only.

It is because 'I' carries this meaning for him that the most obvious candidate for the office of cause of Descartes—his parents—fails after all to pass the test. I am the Ghost in the Machine—a thinking thing—so I must be caused by a thinking thing. My parents may have made my body, but *I* am not my body. The bringing into being of my body by my parents did not necessarily bring into being my mind; all my parents did was, as Descartes puts it, merely to 'implant certain dispositions in that matter in which the self—i.e. the mind, which alone I at present identify with myself—is by me deemed to exist' (Descartes, p. 170). So he concludes that God brought him into being.

(5) Descartes, then, begs the question not once but twice over He starts: 'I exist; I must be caused'. By this he means: 'I (= a thinking thing) exist; something is putting out power to conserve me (or even: something created me)'. This way of approaching the matter contains the answer 'God' for two reasons. Only God can create the soul (if you separate soul or mind from body, as Descartes does, and if, further, you deny that parenthood is any more than bodies bringing bodies into being). Again, only God can conserve.

It would be wrong, however, to suggest that Descartes's arguments for God are without merit. This is far from being the case. He must certainly be given credit for the way in which his arguments call attention to certain aspects of belief in God, though they are, admittedly, debatable aspects—for instance, that it involves belief in conservation, and, perhaps, that it may involve a particular view about the nature of human beings, as essentially souls rather than bodies. (The latter is an important point, to which I shall return in Chapter 10.)

It is usually unfair to take the theistic arguments out of their settings in history and in the writings of particular thinkers. Even though, as often as not, they may have had to face criticism in their own day, they generally spoke to those days in a way they cannot to ours. It is not easy always to be properly sympathetic towards the intentions and accomplishments of philosophers in past ages; yet without sympathy their work may be dismissed too quickly and too easily. It is worth saying here that the Argument from Design and the Argument from Religious

Experience, both of which are to be discussed in later chapters, at least as far as understanding them is concerned, put fewer difficulties in the way of a modern reader than does either the Cosmological Argument or the Ontological Argument.

There is a curious argument in the writings of George Berkeley (1685–1753), that we may note briefly. Even more than in the case of Descartes's, this is an argument that is unlikely to make sense, let alone be thought valid, except to, and by, someone who is prepared to accept a whole philosophical system.

What we perceive, says Berkeley, are 'ideas' in the mind. All the perceptible qualities of sensible things are ideas. Descartes, from the fact that the deliverances of the senses are always changing, from the fact that 'our senses deceive us', concludes that we must distrust them. They are weak and fallible, and give us only error and not certainty. We must look elsewhere for sure and certain knowledge. We must look, in fact, to pure reason. Berkeley sees that we cannot thus abandon the senses. We will get nowhere in knowledge without our senses. We must put up with the fact that we see only qualities of sensible things and not their real 'essences'. Indeed, the 'real essence' (substance or substratum) of a thing does not exist. It does not exist because it cannot be perceived. And *to be is to be perceived* (*esse est percipi*), or, in the case of minds themselves, *to be is to perceive*.

All that we perceive are 'ideas' in the mind, not material objects. Ideas can exist only in a mind; so if there were not minds there would not be anything. Ultimate reality is spiritual; that is, it is mind-dependent: it is mental rather than material; it is ideas rather than material things.

Although to be is to be perceived, it does not follow that if there were no human minds nothing would exist. There would still be God's mind, and God is perceiving everything all the time. This is Berkeley's proof of God. He aims to keep as close as possible to commonsense, though the character of some of his writings might not suggest this; and he sees that it would be intolerably paradoxical to say that things go out of existence as soon as we stop perceiving them. Commonsense requires us to believe that there is some continuity about this world in which

F

we live. Berkeley is still convinced that in the case of sensible things to exist is only to be perceived. What then? As he sees it, there must be a God, who is always perceiving everything, and who thus guarantees the world the continuity that we are convinced it has.

Berkeley's philosophy has been summed up in the well-known limerick by Ronald Knox, together with its anonymous Reply.

' There was once a man who said, "God
  Must think it exceedingly odd
    If he finds that this tree
    Continues to be
When there's no one about in the Quad." '

Reply

' "Dear Sir,
  Your astonishment's odd:
  I am always about in the Quad.
    And that's why the tree
    Will continue to be,
Since observed by
      Yours faithfully,
        God." '

Berkeley's philosophy, of which I have presented a very rough version, is subtle and not without ambiguity. Any kind of detailed study of it would be out of place here. However, the common criticism of his argument for God—here as simplified as is the above account of the argument itself—runs somewhat as follows.

Berkeley's philosophy depends on a denial of the everyday distinction between the act of perceiving and the thing perceived. The appearances that things have may depend on us, but there is something not us which has these appearances for us. A thing is not just a bundle of appearances, which we may concede would be mind-dependent. Admittedly, there cannot be a perception unless there is a perceiver—things cannot 'appear to be red' unless they appear to be red to someone. But you cannot say that if there were no one (man or God) perceiving them they would not *be*, i.e. would not *exist*. You can say that if there were no one perceiving them they would not be (i.e. appear to be) red, but not that they would not be at all (i.e. would not exist). This philosopher of commonsense is not commonsensical enough. In short, if we reject Berkeley's belief that to be is to be perceived, the grounds for the specifically Berkeleian proof of God disappear at the same time, and we are thrown back to more usual forms of the Cosmological Argument, already discussed.

CHAPTER 6

Order and Purpose

THE Ontological and Cosmological Arguments are somewhat abstract in character, which makes them, in an age when 'metaphysics' is suspect, initially hard to understand and liable to seem all too obviously fallacious. They may be contrasted in this respect with those theistic arguments which, though not all by any means recent inventions (except perhaps the Argument from Religious Experience), may seem to the modern scientific mind to depend upon considerations of a more congenially empirical character. Of arguments of this latter kind the most familiar is the Teleological Argument, or Argument from Design—sometimes called the Argument *to* Design. Kant called it the Physico–Theological Argument—a name which, though not many later writers have used it, indicates rather well its would-be scientific character: though, as we shall see, the scientific respectability of this argument is only skin-deep.

In its simplest form the argument runs: The order and design observable in the universe suggests a Supreme Orderer or Designer.

The kind of thing that has usually been appealed to as evidence of order is the solar system, with the planets revolving in their predictable orbits, or the human eye, more subtly constructed than the most elaborate camera. It was generally thought important in the heyday of the argument to accumulate as much evidence as possible, on the principle that the more design the more likely a Designer. For instance, in the first half of the nineteenth century, the Bridgewater Treatises, by distinguished divines and men of science, were devoted to an elaborate attempt, volume by volume, to set out the evidence from many different fields of investigation. It is doubtful, however, whether there is any great virtue in the mere accumulation of evidence, or what is taken to be evidence. The strength, and the weakness, of the argument lie in its basic simplicity, not in the complexities that are introduced by the piling of instance upon instance; and its best advocates and critics alike have realized this.

Linked with the notions of design and order is that of purpose (hence the name Teleological Argument—from $\tau\acute{\epsilon}\lambda os$, 'end'). It is not merely, so it is claimed, that the universe exhibits order or design in the sense of orderliness or regularity; it exhibits order or design in the sense of direction to an end. This is the sense of 'order' that is important for the Argument; and it is clear that not all evidence of order in the other sense is equally good evidence of order in this. The problem, as the advocates of the argument in the eighteenth and early nineteenth centuries saw it, was whether the universe made better sense when regarded as the work of a Supreme Planning Mind or as, in Palmerston's phrase, an 'accidental and fortuitous concurrence of atoms'. The issue is not, in fact, as clear-cut as this, as men came to see in the light of Darwin's *Origin of Species* (1859); for evolutionary theory offers a half-way house between purpose and a Supreme Orderer on the one hand and mere fortuitousness on the other. From the point of view of the Theory of Natural Selection what happens, at any rate on the biological level, is certainly not 'meaningless'; but its explanation is to be sought not outside Nature but within Nature. It may well be said that the evolutionary point of view, though it perhaps suggests that the Argument from Design needs re-interpretation, does not dispose of it: not, that is, unless the kind of explanation that comes as an answer to the question, 'Why are things as they are?' rather than to the question, 'How have things come to be as they are?' is ruled out; and it is difficult to see on what grounds this can be done with any finality. What has happened as a result of evolutionary theory is that this 'Why?' question has been crowded out (though, of course, scientists themselves do sometimes ask 'Why?'), not that it has been shown to be a question that cannot be asked. Men tend not to ask it with their former readiness, and this is on the whole no bad thing; but it remains a perfectly proper question.

The Argument from Design, Kant says, deserves always to be mentioned with respect: it is 'the oldest, the clearest, and the most accordant with the common reason of mankind' (Kant (1), p. 520). This did not prevent him from rejecting it, any more than it prevented Hume from doing so. Hume, like Kant, mixes acceptance with rejection, and provides, in his *Dialogues concerning Natural Religion*, what is probably the best case both for and against the Argument from Design. Before we look at what Hume and Kant had to say, there is another philosopher whose views need to be considered—the best-known of those who gave the Argument unqualified support—that somewhat unjustly neglected writer, Paley.

William Paley (1743–1805) wrote highly popular works on natural religion and Christian apologetics, in one of which, *Natural Theology, or Evidences of the Existence and Attributes of the Deity collected from the Appearances of Nature* (1802), he put forward his version of the Argument from Design. He builds up his argument, particularly in the first half of the book, from considerations of anatomy—on the evidence of design that he finds in the animal and human organism. The human eye, in its complexity of construction and suitability to the purpose which it serves, would of itself, according to Paley, be enough to prove the Supreme Designer; though, as it happens, it is far from standing alone.

It is significant that Paley explicitly rejects any appeal to 'the phenomena of the heavens'. He aims to prove God from the order discernible in living things, and especially in human beings. This is a sensible way of proceeding. True, if the universe is ordered by a Supreme Orderer, we may expect to be able to discern evidence of order in its every part. But the kind of order we find in one part need not be the same as that we find in another part. If we accept the principle, laid down forcefully by Hume, that from a given effect one can argue only to a cause great enough to produce just that effect and no more, and if we further accept that human beings are in some intelligible sense 'higher'

than either inanimate things or animals, then the Argument
from Design is obviously likely to be stronger if it is made to
depend principally on order as discerned on the human level
than if the net in which evidence is to be caught is cast more
widely. Paley says: 'My opinion of Astronomy has always been,
that it is *not* the best medium through which to prove the agency
of an intelligent Creator; but that, this being proved, it shows
beyond all other sciences, the magnificence of his operations.'
On the other hand, it might be claimed that Paley throws away
the advantage thus gained every time he says, as he occasionally
does, that his interest is in the *mechanical* aspects of organisms and
that from this point of view there is no difference between human
beings and lower creatures.

My aim in this part of the chapter is to interpret Paley's intentions, and this requires that I should, right away, put in its
proper place that item in his *Natural Theology* that has become,
unfortunately for its author, the best-known part of it—I mean
the notorious analogy of the watch. At the very beginning of the
work Paley writes: 'In crossing a heath, suppose I pitched my
foot against a *stone*, and were asked how the stone came to be
there: I might possibly answer, that, for anything I knew to the
contrary, it had lain there for ever: nor would it perhaps be very
easy to show the absurdity of this answer. But suppose I had
found a *watch* upon the ground, and it should be inquired how
the watch happened to be in that place; I should hardly think of
the answer which I had before given, that, for any thing I knew,
the watch might have always been there. Yet why should not
this answer serve for the watch as well as for the stone? why is
it not as admissible in the second case, as in the first? For this
reason, and for no other, viz. that when we come to inspect the
watch, we perceive (what we could not discover in the stone)
that its several parts are framed and put together for a purpose,
etc.' He proceeds to describe the workings of a watch. Then:
'This mechanism being observed (it requires indeed an examination of the instrument, and perhaps some previous knowledge of
the subject, to perceive and understand it; but being once, as we
have said, observed and understood), the inference, we think, is
inevitable, that the watch must have had a maker; that there

must have existed, at some time, and at some place or other, an artificer or artificers, who formed it for the purpose which we find it actually to answer; who comprehended its construction, and designed its use.' He elaborates upon this theme, and considers objections, and then, in the opening words of his third chapter, says: 'Every indication of contrivance, every manifestation of design, which existed in the watch, exists in the works of nature; with the difference, on the side of nature, of being greater and more, and that in a degree which exceeds all computation.' Just as the 'contrivance' observable in a watch indicates that the watch is the product of a human mind, so the contrivance observable in nature indicates that it, too, is the product of a mind.

This is often represented as containing the kernel of Paley's thought, and criticism of it considered to constitute sufficient refutation of his whole position. This is hardly fair to Paley. The analogy of the watch was not his own invention, and he presents it, it seems to me, as an introduction to the final position he himself wants to maintain rather than as a statement of it. He in fact lays less stress on analogy than is often supposed.

One phrase in the passages I quoted is especially significant: Paley says, of our recognition of purpose in the watch, that this 'requires indeed an examination of the instrument, *and perhaps some previous knowledge of the subject*' [my italics]. In other words, purpose is not something lying all about us to be directly noticed by even the most naïve; it is an aspect of things that we may become conscious of if we reflect about something that we already know fairly well. It is not that we would directly see a watch to be an object made for a purpose, assuming that we had never come across a watch before; it is rather that seeing a particular watch may remind us of what we already know about machinery. Exactly this kind of point is made by Paley about God. *It is when a man believes in God already*, and knows him as the great Designer of the universe, that he may be struck, when he looks at and reflects on various objects in nature, by the way they bear witness to this great Designer. Paley, like others who have attempted the proof of God, did not really think of himself as proving God to the complete unbeliever so much as making things clearer to the man who is a believer already. It is the critics of the theistic proofs who generally interpret them as directed at the un-believer (and as failing in their supposed aim of convincing him), whereas it is doubtful whether for the most part they have been so directed. I have made this point sufficiently often already not to need to insist on it again.

Some common complaints against Paley, then, are misdirected. He does not make the mistake, as some have said he does, of supposing that we could dissociate ourselves from our past experience and by simple inspection, never having seen a manu-factured object before, discover that a watch, unlike a stone, was the work of human hands. Nor, as others have said, does he make the mistake of supposing—assuming now that we do *not* dissociate ourselves from our past experience—that it is legitimate to argue from cases where we know things to be manufactured (we know that there are watchmakers) to cases where we do not have such knowledge (for, on this interpretation of Paley, we do not know, before we are convinced by the argument, that there is a God). On the contrary, what he says is that *just as* a man who knows something about machinery will be impressed, in some frames of mind, when he contemplates a watch, by the efficient way in which it carries out the task of telling the time, so the believer in a Supreme Being who designed and created man, is impressed, in some frames of mind, when he contemplates human anatomy, by the efficient way in which the various parts carry out their functions.

I do not wish to claim that Paley maintains with complete consistency the position that I have been outlining. But on the whole I am convinced that this is what he intended to say. In the Conclusion of the work he acknowledges that for the most part his readers will be people who believe in God anyway. This being so, he asks, what is the value of the arguments that he has presented? 'It does not . . . appear what is gained by researches from which no new opinion is learnt, and upon the subject of which no proofs were wanted.' His answer is significant. What is gained is 'stability' and 'impression'. That is, in the first place, the belief which is already there acquires a firmer basis. 'It is a matter of incalculable use to feel our foundation; to find a support in argument for what we had taken up upon authority.' In the second place, by frequent or continued reflection upon any subject, we may improve the facility with which we fall into a given train of thought. 'In a *moral view*, I shall not, I believe, be contradicted, when I say, that if one train of thinking be more desirable than another, it is that which regards the phenomena of nature with a constant reference to a supreme, intelligent Author. To have made this the ruling, the habitual sentiment of our minds, is to have laid the foundation of every thing which is religious. The world thenceforth becomes a temple, and life itself one continued act of adoration.' So the value of the Argument from Design is, as we might have expected, a religious one. Granted that a man believes in God already, it will be of great benefit to him to reflect upon the evidence of 'contrivance' in the world; for this will have the effect of confirming him in his belief and in a religious attitude to the world. There can hardly be any doubt that Paley is entirely right in this.

The reader is seldom uncertain about what Paley means. He had a gift for illustration. He did not shirk difficulties. He never lost the main thread of his argument. He had, in short, the misfortune to be a good and clear writer, and therefore easy to criticize, where a more obscure writer might have escaped with a reputation for profundity. He did not aim at originality—he was discussing themes much discussed by others—but he perhaps achieved more than he is given credit for. His presentation of the Argument from Design is an impressive one, particularly for the careful way in which through the *Natural Theology* he develops the idea of an ascending order of God's creatures; and for the candid way in which he faces up to the problem of evil and the appearance of chance in Creation; and, too, for his recognition that the solution of such problems is not to be divorced from prior beliefs. 'I have already observed, that, when we let in religious considerations, we often let in light upon the difficulties of nature . . . . The truth is, we are rather too much delighted with the world, than too little . . . . In a religious view (however we may complain of them in every other), privation, disappointment, and satiety, are not without the most salutary tendencies.'

Before we leave Paley there is one further point about his *Natural Theology* that deserves to be noted. I have referred above to the criticism of the Argument from Design based on evolutionary theory. Paley, interestingly, considers a form of this evolutionary criticism and rejects it. He raises some logical points; but what is perhaps his main objection is simply that there is no *evidence* of natural selection—and writing, as he was, well before Darwin's investigations on the Galapagos Islands, he was clearly right to say this.

Kant, in his treatment of the Argument from Design, of which, as we have already noted, he speaks with great respect, considers it, as he considers all the theistic arguments, as an argument intended to prove God to the non-believer. If indeed the argument is taken as an attempt to prove the Christian God then Kant's criticisms do unquestionably demolish it (see Kant (1), pp. 518–24). As he rightly says, this argument, considered in itself, could never prove a creator of the universe, but only an architect —a being who imposes order on material already existing (like the watchmaker), not a being who also first brings the material into existence. And Kant at the same time criticizes the argument for failure to stand on its own feet—for depending on the Cosmological Argument and ultimately on the Ontological Argument. As he says, there is a natural movement of thought from the order and design of the world to its contingency, and from a Supreme Architect to a Necessary Being upholding the universe. Those who make use of the Argument from Design realize that, alone, it does not give them what they want; but they may not realize clearly enough that in developing their thought they are leaving the safe empirical ground on which the Argument from Design appears to rest and taking their stand instead on the very uncertain ground of the Cosmological and Ontological Arguments—which Kant considers himself already decisively to have refuted.

A year or two before Kant's discussion of the argument in his *Critique of Pure Reason*, Hume's *Dialogues concerning Natural Religion* had appeared posthumously (1779). Here we have the fullest account by Hume of his ideas about religion; though it is worth noting that he discussed religion a good deal in other writings—as, indeed, did Kant, in writings other than the *Critique of Pure Reason*.

The origins of religion, as Hume saw them, lay in such ignoble passions as fear or hope of advantage. When men tried to find rational grounds for religious belief the arguments they turned up did not merit an intelligent man's acceptance. (Kant's grounds for rejecting theistic arguments were very different, and altogether more sympathetic to religion: the powers of man's speculative reason are limited, and in particular incapable of attaining knowledge of God—God is the object of faith, not of knowledge. We shall be examining Kant's position more closely in the next chapter.) Hume, indeed, had little patience with religion, and regarded its influence as a bad one. He was convinced that the existence of God could not be proved, not even by the Argument from Design. His attitude towards this argument, however, is not entirely unambiguous; nor did he intend that it should be: his choice of the dialogue form—with no speaker explicitly identified with himself—was surely deliberate. Nevertheless, Hume's views in the *Dialogues* can be discerned with a fair amount of certainty, even without taking into account his other relevant writings.

One of Hume's main concerns in the *Dialogues* is with difficulties involved in the notion of argument by analogy. One chief difficulty, as Hume sees it, springs from the fact, or what he takes to be the fact, that supporters of the Argument from Design attempt to argue from the universe considered as unique and unparalleled. How can any argument by analogy be built up from such a beginning? Argument by analogy is only possible where we have *species*—where we are able to compare together a number of things of the same kind, and argue that as they are similar in some respects so they may be similar also in other respects. As the universe is unique and unparalleled, we are naturally not able to compare it with other universes. If, *per impossible*, we knew in the case of other universes that they were created, we might argue that this one, which resembles them in certain respects, was also created. (Hume sometimes presents the argument as an attempt to argue from the universe as *effect* to God as its *cause*: an illustration of the tendency that Kant, as we noted, called attention to—the tendency of the Argument from Design to move over into the Cosmological Argument.) In short, the Argument from Design, which pretends to be an argument by analogy, is not really an argument by analogy at all.

I do not think that the supporter of the Argument from Design need argue in the way Hume represents him as doing; and Paley, for one, does not argue in this way. The argument need not depend upon consideration of the universe as a whole. It can, and in Paley's case certainly does, begin from particular parts of the universe, claiming to find in the case of each of them (not that Paley puts any great weight on multiplicity of examples; for him, a single good example would do) evidence of Divine contrivance.

This does not by any means dispose of Hume's difficulties about analogy. Throughout the *Dialogues* he calls attention to the unlikenesses between the work of human architects, watchmakers, and so on, and what may be observed in nature. Certainly there is a great deal of unlikeness. But here we may invoke in defence of the Argument from Design a point that by now the reader may find all too familiar. To a Christian believer, evidence of contrivance in nature may seem obvious. To a sceptic like Hume what seems obvious is how very unlike a watch nature is. If the Argument from Design is considered as a proof of God with power to convince the man who is not already disposed to believe in him then of course it must fail—for the sorts of reason Hume gives. To that extent Hume is certainly right. But to the man who is so disposed it may well make better sense.

Too great a claim has undoubtedly been made for this argument. Properly interpreted however it is not without value. It does show what it shows: it ought not to have been thought to show more than it shows. Hume and Kant have made it quite clear that this argument is no valid argument to the existence of the Christian God. But if on other grounds—authority, perhaps, as Paley suggested—someone has come to believe in the existence of God, this argument can certainly, as Paley saw, have considerable religious value for him.

The argument is not dead. Several writers of more recent date, notably F. R. Tennant (1866–1957), have attempted this kind of empirical approach to the question of knowledge of God.

I want now to examine the claim that the Argument from Design is *scientific*. Of course, no one is likely to suggest that it is in all respects so; this would be highly implausible. But, as we have noted earlier, this argument does retain a certain appeal to the extent that it may be thought to be congenial to a scientific outlook, as the Ontological and Cosmological Arguments are not. I am not saying that even if on examination we were to find that the argument is indeed scientific there would be any particular merit in this; there are more ways of looking at things than the scientific, and merely to be in conformity with a particular manner, however important that manner may be, is not of itself ground for praise. Scientism is not enough. In any case, as we shall see, the argument is not as scientific as it may look.

The best way to approach this claim is by examining not the course of the argument itself but the proposition that is arrived at as its conclusion. This is the proposition: There is a Supreme Orderer, who has arranged the universe in an ordered way. Let us call this proposition the deistic hypothesis—'hypothesis', because we are now supposing the advocate of the Argument from Design to be a kind of scientist and thus able to offer no more than a scientist would offer; that is, neither a categorical assertion nor an *a priori* principle, but an empirical hypothesis to account for what he has observed—in this case order in the universe.

What exactly is involved in claiming that the deistic hypothesis is scientific? The marks of a scientific hypothesis are several in number, but for our present purposes it is enough to note that a scientific hypothesis has the characteristic of being empirically testable, and falsifiable by the finding of a negative instance: failure to conform to this criterion will be sufficient reason for denying the name scientific to the deistic hypothesis.

The deistic hypothesis is not empirically testable. If we ask the advocate of the argument what sort of empirical evidence he wishes to adduce his reply will undoubtedly be, 'Evidence of order'. What is order? To say of things that they are ordered is to say that they possess a pattern, that their parts bear a relation to each other; and to say of events that they are ordered is to say that they are predictable, not unexpected. All this means

order is subjective

nothing unless it is cashed in terms of the *specific* patterns, relations, sequences, in question. The term 'order' is a blanket-term;
it is not itself the name of a property possessed by some sets of
things or events and not by others. And it is a subjective term—
subjective in the sense that it is we who recognize pattern and
sequence. We need not go so far as Kant, who maintained that
the categories in terms of which our experience is ordered are all
imposed by the mind itself and are not in any way objective
features of reality; but it is enough justification for calling order
subjective to note that people see different patterns in the same
set of material. (Consider Rorschach tests with ink blots.) In one
sense of 'experience' all experience might be said to be ordered;
it would not be experience if it were not. One might ask: What
would disordered experience—*completely* disordered experience—
be like? In this sense, simply to say that the universe, or our
experience of the universe—in the present case it comes to the
same thing—is ordered, would be to say nothing. What are of
interest to the scientist are the specific relations and sequences
that he finds in the universe. What he has to say about these is
open to empirical investigation. To say that what the scientist
is *really* seeing is 'order' is obviously true, but uninformative.   *e.g? order in clouds*

doesn't show args scientific

   The natural theologian, in claiming that the universe exhibits
order, is doing one of three things, none of which achieves the
end we are at the moment supposing him to be aiming at, viz.
the development of a *scientific* argument for God. (1) He may be
uttering what he intends to be a truism—the truism, just noted,
that our experience is ordered experience. It must be; we cannot   *we impose order*
help perceiving things in terms of pattern and sequence. This
truism would be not an empirical or scientific proposition, but
an analytic one. (2) He may be claiming to lay bare a distinguishable feature of the universe, its possession of the specific *empirical*
property of being ordered. There is no such property. In this
sense, to say that the universe is ordered is to speak in shorthand:
to be ordered means to possess specific patterns and sequences;
but it is not itself the name of a specific pattern or sequence on a
level with the rest. (3) He may be totally identifying himself with
the scientist, in the sense that in saying the universe is ordered

he means only that it possesses the specific patterns and sequences that scientists have so far discovered and will in the future discover. To this extent, he is keeping well within the limits of the empirical. But if he stops there he will not be a natural theologian. To him, this identification with the scientist can only be a jumping-off place from which to argue to God. In proceeding, as he must, to argue that the observable order of the universe is not adequately explained unless in terms of a Supreme Orderer, he is leaving the realm of the empirical, and the present-day scientist will not follow him.

Two further difficulties may be mentioned. Scientific hypotheses do not generally try to account for everything. What does try to account for everything—as does the deistic hypothesis — is probably better classified as a metaphysical than as a scientific hypothesis. Also, a generally acknowledged feature of scientific method is that where there is more than one way of accounting for the same facts one ought to adopt the simpler. There is, as it happens, an alternative to the deistic hypothesis, which says what it says, but is simpler, in what is to the natural theologian the fatal respect that it does not mention an orderer. The deistic hypothesis runs: There is a Supreme Orderer who has arranged the universe in an ordered way. The alternative runs, simply: The universe is arranged in an ordered (or orderly: 'ordered' slightly implies an orderer) way.

I conclude, then, that the claim that the Argument from Design is a scientific argument cannot be substantiated. This was, perhaps, only to be expected. It is not the job of science to prove God, and scientists today do not operate with the concept of God, whatever may have been the case in past centuries. They have no need of that hypothesis. Religion has never played very effectively the role of pseudo-science that has sometimes been thrust upon her, and both science and religion stand to gain by the recognition that each may travel faster alone. Not that I think there is a serious conflict between science and religion. The possibility of conflict exists when religion is regarded as a kind of (bad) science, or when science is regarded as a kind of substitute religion. The conflict becomes altogether less serious— I do not know that it can ever totally disappear—when the limits of each are more precisely laid down. They do not ask the same kind of question.

Although the Argument from Design is not a scientific argument it does still have, putting it vaguely, scientific connexions. It remains true that this argument implies that empirical evidence is somehow relevant to the question of proof of God. This can certainly not be said of the Ontological Argument; and only in a rather remote sense can it be said of the Causal Arguments. It seems to me that while empirical considerations could never establish the existence of a transcendent God, they must indeed be relevant to any such attempt, though the way in which they are relevant needs careful definition. A few remarks ought perhaps to be made about this.

There is something of a conflict in religious writing between two points of view. Neither, I think, can be abandoned altogether by the Christian believer (though the attempt is sometimes made), and yet they seem mutually incompatible. (a) On the one hand, there is the line of thought that runs: God is infinite, and so quite beyond the finite. God is, in the words of Rudolf Otto (1869–1937), 'The Wholly Other'. If finite human minds try to comprehend God, they are bound to fail. All they can hope for is to grasp something which they interpret, perhaps wrongly, as a manifestation of God; they can never grasp God himself. (b) On the other hand, there is the line of thought that runs: Men have throughout history claimed knowledge of God, even though they have not usually claimed anything like complete knowledge. This must be the starting point. This claim ought to be accepted; and instead of denying that the finite can comprehend the infinite, we ought to begin from the fact that clearly the finite *does* in some degree comprehend the infinite. Men have been convinced that they have knowledge of God. The question is: whence does that knowledge come? On the principle that all knowledge comes originally through sense experience—a principle acknowledged not only by the British Empiricists but by Kant and by Aquinas—we seem bound to answer: knowledge of God comes somehow through sense experience; or, to put it more mildly—for a quite general, even vague, connexion is all we need—sense experience can be relevant to knowledge of God. To some extent belief in God is, I should claim, susceptible of support by evidence of a quite ordinary, empirical kind—somewhat as we may gain fuller knowledge of a writer as we read more of his books. But such evidence can never function unaided as *proof* of God's existence for someone who does not already believe in him.

If the theologian starts by laying it down that finite minds, because finite, cannot comprehend the infinite, he arrives at the view of God as unknowable; and there have been some distinguished expressions of such religious agnosticism. If the theologian starts by accepting the widespread conviction that knowledge of God is possible he may arrive at the view that sense experience, as the basic source of human knowledge, must be relevant to knowledge of God. The chief significance of the Argument from Design lies in the way in which it brings out this issue.

CHAPTER 7

Religion and Morality

WE HAVE now examined the Ontological Argument, the Cosmological Argument, and the Argument from Design. These, though the most important, are not the only arguments for the existence of God. In particular, there is also the Moral Argument.

The Moral Argument can be understood in more than one way. It can be taken as an argument of broadly the same type as the three standard or traditional arguments just named—that is, as a piece of discursive reasoning in which, ostensibly, from premises either about the concept of God or about features of the world a conclusion is drawn of the form, 'Therefore, God exists'. But the version of the Moral Argument that is best known is that of Kant, and in its Kantian form it is of a different kind, and can be taken as offering a new approach to the question whether religion has a rational basis. Kant's Moral Argument is, to use his own terminology, a 'transcendental' argument.

The term 'transcendental', which is a somewhat elusive one, is contrasted with 'empirical'. Kant aimed to construct a transcendental metaphysics, in the sense of a system which would lay bare the necessary conditions of the possibility of experience. The Moral Argument is a transcendental argument in the sense that it endeavours to show that the existence of God is a necessary condition of morality. Morality is the starting point, and it is from morality that one may argue to religion. One argues to it not in the sense of showing that morality is dependent upon or subordinate to religion, but in the sense of showing that belief in God is necessary for making sense of moral experience.

Immanuel Kant was born in 1724 at Königsberg in East

Prussia, the son of a pious saddler. He spent all his life in his native city, where he was professor of logic and metaphysics at the University and where he died in 1804. His involved and dry writings give little clue to his character, which was a good deal less austere than his style. He was fond of company, an entertaining lecturer, deeply interested in the welfare of his students and well liked by them. Religion was a dominating intellectual interest of Kant's, and his contribution to the philosophy of religion is of the very greatest importance: he has, indeed, been accused of having invented the subject.

We have already seen that Kant rejected the Ontological Argument, the Cosmological Argument, and the Argument from Design. These were the theistic arguments that he found chiefly in use. They seemed to him to be the only arguments, in the sense of would-be demonstrative proofs, that could possibly be offered for the existence of God—and they all seemed to him to be invalid. 'Speculative reason', according to Kant, is not capable of proving God's existence. The operations of the speculative reason are limited to the 'phenomenal' world—the world of things as we experience them; whereas God belongs in what he called the 'noumenal' world—the world of things-in-themselves, things as they really are. Kant did not consider that reason is utterly powerless to establish the existence of God. Speculative reason may be powerless, but not reason in another sense. It is through what Kant called the practical reason that conviction of God's existence may come. In the development of this line of thought we have his version of the Moral Argument. (Fundamental to Kant's philosophy is this extremely difficult distinction between sensible phenomenal reality, which is determined by the *a priori* forms of human sensibility and understanding, and noumenal, purely intelligible, reality, which lies behind sensible reality and which is in general beyond sense or understanding yet which can be grasped by reason when reason is functioning as the moral faculty.)

To understand Kant we need to bear in mind that his attitude to religion was in a sense intensely rationalistic. He was not attracted by the institutional side of Christianity, nor by its mystical side. Also, mere belief in historical facts about the origins of Christianity seemed to him to be worthless from a religious point of view. Again, mere acceptance of religious beliefs on Scriptural authority he thought indefensible. His approach to religion was intellectualistic. He considered that we must interpret Scripture in terms of the principles of natural religion, and more especially in terms of moral principles. He deplored 'enthusiasm'—no doubt in reaction against his up-bringing among Pietists—and thought little of public worship, and as little of private: he considered that any man would be ashamed to be found upon his knees in prayer alone.

For Kant the Moral Argument was not a demonstrative proof. In ruling out speculative reason as an instrument for gaining knowledge of God Kant gave up any claim, and indeed wish, to be able to offer logically compelling proofs in this matter. As he had written in an early work (an essay published in 1762): 'It is very necessary that one should be convinced of God's existence; but not so necessary that one should prove it' (see Webb, p. 34). The so-called Moral Argument—at least in the form given to it by Kant—is not, then, strictly speaking, intended to be a proof of God. It is rather an attempt to suggest that religion and morality are bound up together in a complex way, one effect of which is that from considering what morality is, we are led to a belief in the existence of God as what Kant calls 'a postulate of the practical reason'. For Kant the 'postulates' of practical reason are not mere assumptions or presuppositions. They are necessary conditions of the possibility of the Moral Law. And that there is an absolute Moral Law is for him not open to question. The status of Kant's 'postulates' is then altogether more exalted than that of mere assumptions.

His view of religion was one which hardly distinguished it from morality. He more than once defined religion as the recognition of all our duties as divine commands. The religious man is not the man who holds a set of metaphysical beliefs; he is a certain sort of moral man. It is not that he holds some things to be duties that non-religious people do not—duties to God as opposed to duties to one's fellow-men, for instance. The religious man recognizes the same duties as does everybody else—neither more nor less. The difference is that he recognizes them as possessing the special character of divine commands. Kant's moral philosophy has a markedly biblical flavour, as far as its expression is concerned, and clearly this is a legacy of his Pietist upbringing. 'Act only on that maxim whereby thou canst at the same time will that it should become a universal law'—so runs the first formulation of his famous Categorical Imperative, the moral law binding upon all rational creatures (Kant (2), p. 38); and in his slipping here into the second person singular the echo of the 'Thou shalt ... Thou shalt not ...' of the Decalogue is unmistakable.

Kant's attitude to the Moral Law, which is such a central concept in his philosophy, was one of reverence, and in a well-known passage he couples it with something else towards which people have often felt emotions of a religious or quasi-religious character. 'Two things fill the mind with ever new and increasing admiration and awe, the oftener and the more steadily we reflect on them: *the starry heavens above and the moral law within*' (Kant (2), p. 260). These phrases sum up, indeed, the chief interests of Kant's intellectual life: physics and morals; and, in particular, the problem of free will, which seemed to be posed ever more seriously as the physicists offered their own kind of explanation for more and more events. The interest in morality came no doubt from his childhood religious training; the interest in physics from his studies as a young man: and the earlier training may be said to have proved the dominant influence, both in the sense that his devotion to moral philosophy, as far as his publications are concerned, outlived his devotion to physics, and in the perhaps more important sense that, as we have noted, his attitude even to the objects of his science was a quasi-religious one.

Kant is a complex thinker, and there is always a danger in considering part of his views in isolation from the rest. He himself had an almost pathological addiction to what he called 'architectonic', or the systematic arrangement of his material; and to isolate particular items of his thought from the pattern which they help to build up would not have met with his own approval. But it must be done, and we shall now leave these more general considerations about Kant's religious philosophy and turn to look more closely at his Moral Argument proper.

Kant linked together the concepts of God, freedom, and immortality. These are the themes of metaphysics. Also, he presented belief in these three things as postulates of the practical reason. The practical reason is the moral faculty, so to call something a postulate of the practical reason is a way of saying that it is something that we are compelled to postulate in order to make sense of morality. Kant's view was, indeed, that morality could not exist without God, freedom, and immortality; and that if we begin from the fact—it seemed to him a fact—of a real, objective, Moral Law we are bound to postulate these three things. This is not demonstrative proof, but this postulation is certainly a rational procedure. Demonstrative proof is not the only kind of rational justification of a belief.

Kant's point is that there is no sense in morality—no sense in using terms like 'duty'—unless there is moral freedom. 'Ought implies can.' That is, it makes no sense to say of someone that he ought to do something unless it is in his power to do that thing. Unless we are free to do or to refrain from doing at least some of the things we do, morality has no meaning. So Kant would argue. Kant begins from the conviction that morality does have a meaning—that it is indeed the most important thing in human life—and it is out of his reflection on morality that he considers himself bound to postulate freedom, in spite of any theoretical arguments that suggest that our apparent consciousness of freedom is illusory.

But this postulate alone is not enough. The perfect good for man must, Kant holds, include both virtue and happiness; virtue is supreme, but nevertheless virtue together with happiness (that is, happiness *on condition of* virtue) is better than virtue alone. Now, in this world, as we know from experience, virtue is not always crowned with happiness. We see at once that it is necessary, if we are to preserve the beliefs that the perfect good for man consists in both virtue and happiness and that the perfect good is attainable by all men, that we should postulate some other world than this. Kant argues as follows. The Moral Law commands us to pursue virtue, but true virtue, which Kant equates with holiness, is beyond the powers of a human being to attain at any given moment and must be understood rather as an unending progress towards an ideal. And such an unending progress is only possible if we suppose 'the unending duration of the existence and personality of the same rational being, which is called the immortality of the soul' (Kant (2), p. 218). To deny immortality is to deny meaning to morality.

The third postulate, that of God, follows close upon the second. For a man to achieve happiness implies harmony between his wishes and the processes of Nature; for a man's happiness consists in everything happening in accordance with his wish and will. Clearly, we do not ourselves have the power to ensure Nature's co-operation. We must therefore postulate a Being who is the cause of Nature and who has the power to see to it that Nature co-operates in ensuring that happiness does follow virtue. Only a Being who acts by intelligence and will can do this, and such a Being is God. Unless God exists there can be no certainty that the connexion of happiness with virtue in which man's perfect good seems to consist will be realized, and unless it is realized morality once more loses its meaning.

As Kant presents it (in the second of his three *Critiques*, the *Critique of Practical Reason*), the case seems an impressive one, though there is a difficulty about accepting the view that the perfect good is actually attainable by all men, a difficulty that I shall return to later (in Chapter 10). What is most striking about Kant's views on morality is his insistence on the objectivity of the Moral Law, its absolute bindingness on all rational creatures and its independence of their own feelings or inclinations. He certainly considered that this, his starting point—the absoluteness or objectivity of the Moral Law—was itself no mere matter of personal opinion; that it was, in fact, something that no man who seriously considered the matter could possibly deny. The fact is, however, that it can without contradiction be denied, and many people would deny it. Something further will be said about this in the next section of the chapter, but, in the meantime, it is enough to note that as long as there can be fundamental lack of agreement on the starting point of Kant's argument, the argument itself will not convince everybody. (To use terms like 'objective' or 'absolute' in discussing morals is probably to invite confusion; for they are highly ambiguous. I shall postpone any attempt to examine these terms more fully until later in the chapter.)

It would be wrong to press this point as a criticism of Kant. Logical rigour, and universal validity, may belong to the products of the speculative reason, but such descriptions seem less in place when we are discussing the products of the practical reason. Kant, indeed, illustrates the point that I have been concerned to stress throughout—that an argument for the existence of God is only likely to carry conviction to someone who believes in God already. And Kant, although, as we have noted, not conspicuously attached to the observance of Christian practices, was certainly a believer in God.

It may be doubted, however, whether he had a completely clear recognition of the connexion between his own belief in God, early instilled in him and never lost, and his conviction of the cogency of his Moral Argument for God's existence. He certainly had no such clear recognition as Anselm had of the connexion between *his* faith in God and his conviction of the cogency of the Ontological Argument. For Kant, morality came first in importance and religion second. His chief intention in the so-called Moral Argument was to guarantee morality. As a believer in God, it was natural for him to seek for this guarantee where he did. Had he been an atheist, he would have sought elsewhere. This is a somewhat unreal speculation, as Kant, if he had indeed been an atheist, might never have held the views about morals that he did. In fact, to return to the point that I made earlier, for him religion and morality were bound up together in a highly complex way. He learned them together, and never succeeded in separating them; indeed, never wished to. But, for all that his views on morals would never have been what they were but for his childhood religious training, if he had been compelled to discard the conscious adherence to one or the other there can be little doubt that he would have clung to the moral theory and let religion go. His interest in religion was sincere, and his writings on religious philosophy are, as I remarked above, among the greatest; yet it is impossible to read him without feeling that for him God's real importance was as a cog in the machine of his moral philosophy. Kant is not interested in the proof of the

existence of God for the sake of the clarification of belief in God,
as were Anselm or Aquinas.

Against this must be set his recognition that knowledge of God
is a matter of a man's moral and religious experience rather than
something that he convinces himself about by speculative reasoning. By Kant's time there was a tendency for the great theistic
proofs of Anselm and Aquinas to be divorced from the faith in
God with which their original proponents had essentially linked
them and to become mere dry logical exercises. The effect of
Kant's denial of right to speculative reason to prove the existence
of God, backed by his devastating criticism of the logic of those
arguments, was to work itself out in the shape of the post-
Kantian interest in 'religious experience' and in the development
of the so-called Argument from Religious Experience, which we
are to examine in the next chapter.

Kant has been criticized by modern Thomists for his rejection
of Aquinas's arguments. But it could plausibly be argued that
Kant, despite his rejection of the arguments themselves, was in
reality restoring the basic insight of Aquinas (and of Anselm),
which is in some ways more important than the arguments
themselves—the insight, by now so familiar to the reader, that
faith in God and proof of God go hand in hand. If no one who
is not a believer in God already is likely to be convinced by the
theistic arguments anyway, it seems relatively unimportant
whether, considered as pieces of logic, these arguments have
flaws. Kant, in his discussion of the theistic proofs in the *Critique
of Pure Reason*, aimed at disposing of false claims to knowledge of
God and replacing them by faith in God. Mere logic will not
give a man sure and certain knowledge of God. What is appropriate in this case is belief or faith—based, said Kant, on moral
principles. The importance of faith Anselm, and to a lesser extent
Aquinas, also saw.

The paradoxical thing about Kant's religious philosophy is,
indeed, the way in which it combines a stress on reason with a
stress on faith. Kant was in a sense a rationalist in religion, as
we have noted already, unwilling to accept religious belief on
authority, and wanting to subject it all to the test of rational, and
in particular moral, principles. At the same time, he was insistent

that belief in God is not something that can be arrived at by mere speculative reason. Only the practical reason, working upon a man's already acquired store of moral experience (and for Kant, we must remember, 'moral' and 'religious' were never sharply distinguished), in particular his experience of the Moral Law, can provide it. Though we may indeed say that what it provides is not proof but a postulate, it remains true that in Kant's sense of the term a postulate is as good as a proof.

The present discussion of the Moral Argument raises the whole question of the relation between religion and morality. It is a question to which very different answers have been given. At one extreme is the view which has received an often quoted expression in Matthew Arnold's remark that religion is 'morality touched by emotion'. At the other extreme of such a virtual identification of religion and morality is the view of Kierkegaard, who held that between the moral and the religious life there is a gulf which few succeed in crossing, and that to enter fully upon the religious life may involve turning one's back upon the practice of 'ordinary' or 'mere' morality. Kant's own view, which amounts to a subordination of religion to morality, comes somewhere between these extremes. So also does the view, the opposite of Kant's, which is perhaps the most widely held of all—the view that subordinates morality to religion, and seeks the theoretical justification of moral principles in the invocation of 'the will of God' or some other religious notion. This last mentioned view will repay a brief examination.

It is sometimes thought that the absoluteness of moral principles can only be guaranteed if they are somehow derived from the will of God. This is a mistaken view. It is sometimes so put as to suggest that the only alternative to principles laid down by the divine will is an anarchy of complete relativism or 'subjectivism', where 'right' and 'wrong' are defined only in terms of what each user of the words happens to like or dislike. Such a suggestion is absurd. The terms 'absolute' and 'relative' (and also 'objective' and 'subjective') are ambiguous. In calling a moral principle absolute (e.g. the principle of keeping promises, or telling the truth, or helping others in distress) we may intend either or both of two things. We may mean to claim that it is without exception, or unconditional, or binding in all circumstances. Let us call this absoluteness of status. Or we may mean to claim that it is not dependent, not man-made, not a mere rule devised by society for promoting its own welfare. Let us call this absoluteness of origin. Kant himself believed moral principles to be absolute in both these senses; but his interest was perhaps more in absoluteness of status than in absoluteness of origin.

The belief that, if they are to be absolute, moral principles must be derived from the will of God seems to depend largely upon a confusion of these two senses of 'absolute'. The claim seems to be that absoluteness of status requires absoluteness of origin. This is not so. The way in which a given moral principle may be supposed to have originated—in a divine command, in a 'dictate of reason', in social evolution, in individual opinion— has no necessary bearing upon the question whether it has absoluteness of status. If the claim that the absoluteness of moral principles can only be guaranteed if they are derived from the will of God means that only an absolute origin can guarantee an absolute status it is plainly mistaken.

This is not the only difficulty faced by this claim. It is doubtful, in any case, whether absoluteness of origin is itself compatible with derivation from the will of God. If moral principles were indeed derived from the will of God we might well consider them *not* to possess absoluteness of origin. They are absolute only if they are independent of any will, even the divine will.

It may be objected to what has just been said that whereas to attempt to derive moral principles from any individual human will, or from society, would indeed be to destroy their absoluteness, this cannot be so if they are derived from God. Is God not Creator—and, if so, must he not be creator of moral principles? Again, is not God worshipped as all-good, so that his will, unlike that of any other being, always issues in decisions and commands that are good, and never in any that are evil: which surely means that to say that moral principles derive from God must be only another way of saying that they are absolute?

There is some force in this objection. But it does not survive close examination. We may acknowledge that God as Creator has created, among other things, moral principles. It does not follow however that he has created them directly; he may have created them merely in the sense that he has created man, and has left man to develop for himself the principles that he (man) has come to call moral. God, in creating man with free will, may not have determined the precise form that those principles have taken. As far as the other half of the objection is concerned, we must reply that, although God is worshipped as all-good, this does not rule out the possibility of his being supposed evil on at least some occasions. ('God is good' is not usually taken as analytic: at least, no reputable theologian has ever, as far as I know, treated it as if it were.) Indeed, it is just this possibility which is one of the things that goes to make the Problem of Evil (to be discussed in Chapter 9) such a serious difficulty for the reflective religious believer. It seems to me, though this might be disputed, to be a matter of contingent fact, not a matter of necessity, that God's will is always good. If this is so, the grounding of moral principles in the will of God gives them a less secure foundation than is generally supposed. (If anyone were disposed to insist that it is necessary and not contingent that God is good he would not, I think, save the situation; for then 'God is good' is probably vacuous. (See, on this, Martin, Chaps. 3-4.)

The main point, to return to it, is that any attempt to make moral principles dependent on anything, even the divine will, seems to be incompatible with the claim that they are absolute in origin. If they are absolute, in this sense, they are independent. It is not my present purpose to answer the question whether moral principles in fact are absolute in either of the senses distinguished above; my point is simply that it is inconsistent for someone who maintains that they are absolute in origin to maintain at the same time that they are derived from the divine, or from any other, will. Yet, strangely, far from this being recognized, some people seem to think that it would be inconsistent *not* to maintain a divine origin for moral principles if they are also held to be absolute. Closer reflection on our actual moral practice should, however, disabuse them of this mistake. We are prepared, if the occasion demands, to make use of a moral test in order to establish the genuineness of an alleged divine command.

('You only think that God is commanding you to do that. You must be mistaken. It's immoral; so God can't be commanding it.') No intelligent religious person will obey the will of God just because it is the will of God; but only because he also believes that God can be relied upon to desire of us only that which is right. If we thought God commanded evil, we should not think it right to obey him. This shows that we do not in fact behave as if 'moral' were synonymous with 'commanded by God'. If these were synonymous, there would be no point, as in fact there clearly is a point, in saying that God only commands what is right; for in that case to say this would be only to say 'God commands what he commands'. No; the attempt to derive moral principles from religion, where this means from the will of God, will not work.

This is, admittedly, not the only way in which morality may be claimed to be subordinate to religion, but it is perhaps the commonest, and it is sufficient example. There seems no doubt that moral principles had their historical origin independently of religion, though the two have come to be closely intertwined, and in Christianity much religious teaching might equally well be called moral teaching. But there is no logical priority of one over the other. There is nothing inconsistent about being a moral man and an atheist. The extent to which Christian teachers and preachers have assumed proprietorial interests in morality is to be deplored. Certainly, in many respects, the ethics of Christianity show an advance over other systems of ethical teaching; but to speak, as some Christians do, as if only the professing, or even professional, Christian had the right to make pronouncements on moral matters is indefensible.

It is sometimes said that morality is dependent on religion in a psychological, not a logical sense. That is, the Christian has in his religion something which provides a drive or force in his moral life—something that is not available to the non-believer. This may well be the case; and I have no quarrel with this particular version of the view which subordinates morality to religion. But this, it is clear, has no bearing on the impropriety of subordinating morality to religion in a logical or theoretical sense.

CHAPTER 8

Religious Experience

INTEREST in 'religious experience' is, as I pointed out in Chapter 2, of comparatively recent origin; it is largely post-Romantic Revolution. In particular, an appeal to religious experience in the proof of God's existence is something that would not have occurred to Anselm, or Aquinas, or even Descartes. Not that these men had no 'religious experiences'. But they made no use in argument of the concept of religious experience as this has been understood in the nineteenth and twentieth centuries.

As it has come to be used, 'religious experience' means some kind of emotional experience or condition, or an experience or condition that is somehow both emotional and cognitive. To 'experience religion', to use a phrase that once had some currency, means to be 'converted'; and conversion has come to be thought of to a large extent in emotional terms. This, as I have said, is not how Anselm or Aquinas would have looked at the matter; and in this they were certainly right. A parallel may be drawn with aesthetics. The feeling-tone of aesthetic appreciation is irrelevant to aesthetic value—though this, admittedly, might not be universally accepted. What matters is the work of art itself, and it neither gains nor loses in value on account of the emotional reactions of those who contemplate it. In much the same way, it might be said of religion that what matters is the object of religious attitudes—God—not those attitudes themselves. Too much concentration on 'the experience of the religious man', where this means, as it commonly does, his inner emotional states, is a mistake; as is, in the other field, too much concentration on aesthetic feelings at the expense of works of art themselves.

I am far from wishing to deny all value to the study of religious experience. It has great value. What seems to me unwise is too exclusive a preoccupation with it, and, in particular, too exclusive a preoccupation with the idea that the best, or even the only, way of getting knowledge of God is by studying our own, or, as far as we can, other people's feelings, emotions, attitudes. To take another parallel, it is as if we were to claim that the way to understand another person, or even perhaps the way to find out whether he exists, is not to observe that person himself and consider the significance of what he does, but to analyse our own emotional reactions when we find ourselves in his presence. This latter procedure does, of course, have its point. Some very forceful person may induce in us a particular kind of psychological state— apprehension, perhaps—and it may be by noting our own reaction to him that we become aware that he is a forceful person and so learn something important about him. But, certainly, to treat this as the only way of acquiring knowledge of other people's *existence* would be logically absurd (more on this later), and even to treat it as the best way is, at the least, misguided.

It is equally absurd or misguided to claim that God can only, or can best, be known through religious experience—in the sense in which this term is commonly used by those who would make the claim. Yet dissatisfaction with the older theistic proofs has led some Christian theologians and philosophers to claim just this; and at the present time there is a widespread fascination with 'religious experience', and a widespread belief that it is here—and only here—that the basis of a rational argument for God's existence, or even, some might say, of the truth of religion as a whole, is to be found. I am writing, I should perhaps say, of a tendency of thought rather than of the views of any particular writer; and for the purposes of this discussion I am taking this tendency to its logical extreme. In practice, there is sometimes a greater readiness than I am allowing here to permit alongside religious experience as the chief source of knowledge of God a place also—it may be a comparatively subordinate place—for other things, like, for instance, 'revelation', or even perhaps one or more of the standard theistic proofs in modified form.

There are a number of questions that we need to examine.

First, what is religious experience? Secondly, what are its origins? Thirdly, how can we tell a genuine from a non-genuine religious experience? Fourthly, and the other questions are all preliminary to this, is it possible to infer the existence of God from the fact, if it is a fact, that people have religious experiences?

Let us begin with the first of these questions. What is religious experience? To experience something is to have something happen to you. This, I take it, is how the expression is generally used. 'I had a strange experience late one night years ago when I was walking along Lathbury Road. . . .' The Oxford English Dictionary says of the verb 'experience', among other things, 'to have experience of; to meet with, to feel, suffer, undergo'. To have a religious experience is to have something happen to you that has, or is considered by you to have, religious significance. What sort of significance is religious significance? In the Christian, or at least the Protestant Christian, tradition, this generally means that the experience is thought to be 'directly' of God, or that it leads to conviction of the existence of God, or to the conviction that God really does possess such-and-such attributes which we have been told he possesses. Or it may be an experience which brings home to the experient his own moral shortcomings, or both does this and suggests some remedy for them.

Religious experience has come to be understood as some kind of 'inner', emotional experience. To quote the dictionary again, this time on the noun 'experience': 'In religious use: A state of mind or feeling forming part of the inner religious life; the mental history (of a person) with regard to religious emotion'.

The term 'religious experience' is often equated with 'experience of God'. If we accept this equation, having a religious experience might be said to constitute direct acquaintance with God. If we do not make the equation, knowledge of God involves some further inferential step. On both these versions, religious experience is generally considered to be essentially inner or private—and even, it is sometimes added, incommunicable.

Linked sometimes with the view of religious experience that we are considering is a presentation of religion as something that each man makes for himself, on the basis of his own, personal, experiences. There is often a quite explicit turning of the back upon the tradition which includes under 'religious experience' something that might be called the experience of the Church, which the individual may take over and enter into. Such a tradition is sometimes rejected as offering only a 'second-hand' kind of religion. So, indeed it may; but it need not. An immersing of oneself in traditional religion is itself a kind of religious experience. Admittedly, the 'second-hand' type of religion may call logically for explanation in terms of a first-hand type of religion. It is a mistake, however, to suppose, as I think is sometimes supposed, that a thing that needs such explanation must always be worth less than the thing in terms of which it is explained. Though men may never come to be in Situation B unless other men have first been in Situation A, this does not mean that Situation B must in all cases be written off as no more than a poor copy of Situation A. It may even be something better. To take a different but similar case, a prototype aeroplane is not necessarily of more value, as a practical, usable aeroplane, than the latest machine deriving from it. Quite the reverse. Certainly, Situation B 'depends upon' Situation A ('second-hand' depends upon 'first-hand'); but this is a logical dependence, and nothing follows from it about the respective value in any other sense of A and B: in the present context, nothing follows about their respective religious values.

It is of some importance that the limitations of the common use of 'religious experience' should be recognized. A rational basis, of a kind, for religion might perhaps be found in religious experience, but not in the sense of the term that I have been discussing. The difficulties in the notion of private experiences—especially, of course, if these are claimed to be also incommunicable—as a basis for argument to God's existence are perhaps sufficiently obvious, though I shall bring them out explicitly later in the present chapter. I do not, of course, question the value to the believer himself of a careful analysis of his own experiences; this may indeed help both to make clearer to him what it is that he believes in and to confirm him in that belief.

The notion of religious experience is, unfortunately, ambiguous in more ways than one. Even if, for the sake of argument, we

accept the view of it as a kind of inner, emotional experience—
and let us for ease of future reference now give this view a label;
let us call it the Private Experience View—even if we accept
this view, there are ambiguities within it.

To some, nothing is allowed to count as a religious experience
that is not dramatic or spectacular—involving, perhaps, locutions
or visions. To others, quite ordinary experiences—like the mild
euphoria induced by a summer evening's walk across the fields
after a day of strain in the city—may seem to have religious
significance and to deserve the name of religious experience. This
difference is not unimportant. It bears closely on the question,
which is the next question to be taken up in this chapter,
of the origins of religious experience: a particular suggested natural
origin may seem fairly implausible if we are thinking of religious
experience in the first of the senses just mentioned, but not if we
are thinking of it in the second. Clearly, an argument to the
existence of God based upon the rare, 'abnormal' experiences of
a few individuals, will differ in both presentation and effect from
one based upon relatively everyday experiences that almost
anybody might be supposed to recognize in himself.

Again, Otto's *The Idea of the Holy*, first published in 1917, is
responsible for the view of religious experience as 'numinous' experience, experience of 'the Wholly Other', experience, essentially
indefinable, in which the element of awe plays a large part. Then
again, the influence of Kant has tended towards an understanding
of religious experience in moral terms.

So far we have been noting ambiguities within the Private
Experience View. There is also an ambiguity between this view
itself and what we may call the Public Experience View. To
experience something may indeed be to have something happen
to you, 'to meet with, to feel, suffer, undergo'. But this need not
be understood in 'inner', 'emotional' terms. A man may, as we
sometimes say, live through an experience which changes his life.
Such an experience is frequently fully describable in terms of its
public features. We can, in a sense, take it for granted that
something is going on 'inside' him as well; but we may not
consider that the difficulty, or impossibility, of getting clear what
this is, precludes us from describing his *experience*. 'He was

shipwrecked for seven weeks with nothing to drink but a little rain-water and nothing to eat but a few crabs; and when they rescued him he was so weak he could barely lift his hand.'—'What a terrible experience!' The man himself might be satisfied to describe his experience in terms of what led up to the shipwreck, his surroundings on the atoll, his physical deterioration, etc. How he felt, both he and we may, as I said, be happy to take for granted; emotions are, anyway, notoriously hard to describe. My point is that what he would have provided, by giving such an account in terms of the 'public' elements of the situation, is the sort of thing that we are very often willing to call an account of an 'experience'. An appeal to usage may be successfully made in support of the private sense of 'experience'; but so may it be made in support of the public sense.

An account of a lifetime of 'religious experience' might well be couched in largely 'public' terms. Simply being present at church services is part of a man's religious experience. No doubt the Public Experience View uses 'experience' in a somewhat different sense from that in which the Private Experience View uses it; but neither can legitimately claim to be using the term in its only 'proper' sense. Such a claim could not be made in the case of 'experience' when it does not carry the qualifying adjective 'religious', and there seems no good reason why it should be made when that qualification is present. Any tendency for the Private Experience View to be taken as the only true or proper one, and the Public Experience View to be dismissed as no more than parasitical upon it, is for the theologian an unfortunate one, though he does not always see this. If a rational basis for religion is to be sought for in religious experience, it must be in religious experience understood in a wide sense, in a sense that includes both the private and the public views. If religious belief is made to depend on religious experience where this is understood as something essentially inner, something essentially private, as emotional goings-on in a man's soul not directly observable by anyone else, then its foundations are shaky indeed, as I shall argue later in the chapter.

I want now to turn to the second of the four questions with which we began, that of the origins of religious experience.

An argument to the existence of God from religious experience depends on a certain view about the origins of religious experience. It might, indeed, be said to reduce to nothing more than a view about this. If religious experience can be explained causally in purely natural terms, its value in providing a proof of God will be greatly diminished. Proving God from religious experience, and attempting to show that religious experience has ultimately a divine origin, go hand in hand; or, as I said, may well be the same thing. It is perhaps worth noting that if religious experience can be accounted for in natural terms this does not necessarily totally destroy its value as proof of God: for God might work through natural causes; and, indeed, it would generally be said that he does. However, it would much reduce its value. There would not be much point in both acknowledging that religious experience can be accounted for in terms of natural origins and at the same time appealing to it in the proof of God's existence.

Many religious believers no doubt accept unquestioningly a divine origin of religious experiences. Persons of a more sceptical turn of mind will not be content to do this. Let us consider some of the more important of suggested natural origins. 'Origins' is in some ways an unsatisfactory word here. Some such phrase as 'predisposing conditions' might be better. However, for brevity's sake I shall use 'origins', or even 'causes'. Some of the suggested explanations I am about to list are offered by their advocates primarily as explanations of religious belief, but they can readily be interpreted as explanations also of religious experience. I shall assume throughout this section the Private Experience View, and will postpone further discussion of its shortcomings to the last section of the chapter.

The origins of religious experience may be in sex. So Freud thought, and his suggestion is plausible enough when applied to at least some religious people. There is, it is true, no conclusive empirical evidence in this matter. But then it is difficult to see how there ever could be. And perhaps none of the suggested origins of religious experience that we are to consider is capable of satisfactory demonstration—any more, of course, than are suggestions of divine origin. Certainly, of none of them can it be said that it is plausible if put forward in isolation, or as an explanation of all cases. There is, nevertheless, something to be said for most, though not all, of them; and a view of religion as sublimated sex does seem to make sense as applied to, say, some devout middle-aged spinsters, or some celibate priests devoted to vestments, incense, and Mother Church. The force of Freud's theories about religion lies in their suggestiveness as explanations in some cases—though certainly not, as he himself might have claimed, as universally valid explanations. 'Of course! So that's why,' we may exclaim; and everything suddenly seems clear. Certainly, we may be wrong; we can never be sure that we are right: but this kind of view undoubtedly does supply illumination of a sort.

It can be suggested, secondly, that the origins of religious experience lie in bodily disorder or disease. This is the view held by what William James (1842–1910) called 'medical materialists'. As he says in a typically Jamesian passage: 'Medical materialism finishes up Saint Paul by calling his vision on the road to Damascus a discharging lesion of the occipital cortex, he being an epileptic. It snuffs out Saint Teresa as an hysteric, Saint Francis of Assisi as an hereditary degenerate. George Fox's discontent with the shams of his age, and his pining for spiritual veracity, it treats as a symptom of a disordered colon. Carlyle's organ-tones of misery it accounts for by a gastro-duodenal catarrh' (James, p. 13).

James decidedly rejected medical materialism. 'To plead the organic causation of a religious state of mind ... in refutation of its claim to possess superior spiritual value, is quite illogical and arbitrary, unless one has already worked out in advance some psycho-physical theory connecting spiritual values in general with determinate sorts of physiological change. Otherwise none of our thoughts and feelings, not even our scientific doctrines, not even our *dis*-beliefs, could retain any value as revelations of the truth, for every one of them without exception flows from the state of their possessor's body at the time' (James, p. 14).

It is perhaps not beyond the bounds of possibility that the kind of psycho-physical theory that James found wanting in the views of medical materialists could be furnished. But his main point is that what one might call the religious value of religious experience is not affected by the mere fact that it springs from-this or that bodily condition. Is he right? There is a connexion between unusual bodily conditions and religious experiences (for instance, fasting, together with its purely physiological effects, though neither a sufficient nor a necessary condition of religious experience, is apt to strike us as not unconnected with it); but it does seem to be the case that the value of the experiences can be assessed in isolation from these bodily conditions. So far, it seems, James is right. At the same time, if it were the case—which, of course, has not been established—that religious experience frequently occurs in certain specifiable conditions of bodily disorder, it would surely be right to treat any claims to superior knowledge or insight that might be made by people having religious experiences—particularly if we assume these for present purposes to be rather rare—with a fair degree of suspicion. There is surely a middle way between outright rejection of 'medical materialism' and uncritical acceptance of it. The explanations of medical materialists ought not to be generalized too widely. They do not illuminate all cases. Nevertheless (*pace* James), it might reasonably be claimed that they do seem to illuminate some.

Another origin of religious experience may lie not in bodily disease but in bodily well-being. This may seem not to deserve listing on its own account. Might it not better be included with the previous heading under some such general name as 'bodily condition'? But it does, I think, need a separate heading. People who look for a bodily origin for religious experience almost always look for it in some abnormal or diseased bodily condition. The suggestion that they might also look among normal healthy conditions they might be inclined not to accept. As they see it, religious experience is itself something 'abnormal', or at any rate something out of the ordinary, and its causes must be abnormal or out of the ordinary. In a sense, I suppose, perfect health is probably abnormal and out of the ordinary; but not in the sense wanted here. If we were to make use of the notion of general bodily condition—a notion, that is, including under it both abnormal and normal conditions—we should indeed be laying ourselves open to James's attack. If any bodily condition whatever could be appealed to on some occasion as the predisposing cause of religious experience, then the appeal to bodily condition would have no explanatory force. To the extent that that appeal is made only to a diseased condition to the exclusion of the contrasting healthy condition there is at least the possibility of explanation. What is lacking, as we saw, is a proper empirical investigation, without which this 'explanation' has no very firm basis; but, as I have already suggested, such an investigation ought not to be in principle impossible.

As I hinted earlier, much of the difficulty here hinges on the ambiguity of the expression 'religious experience'. If no experience were to be accepted as religious unless, among other things, it was somehow remarkable, dramatic, spectacular, then the suggestion that bodily well-being might be a (or the) cause of religious experience will seem quite implausible. But if a much more ordinary feeling that God's in his heaven and all's right with the world be admitted as a religious experience, the suggestion that its origin may lie in bodily well-being will not seem so implausible.

Yet another origin of religious experience may be found in drugs—mescalin, for instance, or lysergic acid. This whole subject—which bears very directly on our central theme, the place of reason in religion—deserves to be treated at length. I shall merely note here that whether taking drugs is to be admitted as one of the causes of religious experience will depend, in part at least, on the content of the experiences so induced, and thus, once again, on our definition of 'religious experience'. (The content of the experiences induced by mescalin in different subjects can in fact vary considerably. See on this Zaehner, Appendixes A and B.)

We may note, as another possible cause, mental well-being; this may be what James calls 'persistent enjoyment'. Much the same considerations apply here as to the case of bodily well-being.

Emotional stress is another, and an obvious, predisposing condition.

Crises of personal life, or natural calamities: these, too, provide predisposing conditions, and of a somewhat different kind from those noted already.

A sense of sin or of guilt—this might, but need not, turn out to be the same as the case of emotional stress—is an equally obvious cause. It might be said that a sense of sin is less a cause of religious experience than a component of it. (Much the same comment might be made in the case of some of the other suggested origins. And so might much the same reply. . . .) Certainly, this will often be so; but there will be other cases where it seems more natural to consider it, as I am doing here, as the origin, or part-origin, of the experience. The question of guilt or sin, which is so central in the Christian religion, deserves a much fuller treatment than I can give it here; and I am prepared to acknowledge that I am probably not doing it justice in including it in the present list as simply one suggestion alongside others about the origins of religious experience. It might be argued by some, though I should not myself so argue, that in the Christian system conviction of sin together with repentance is a necessary condition of having a genuine religious experience. But I shall not pursue this point further.

It has been suggested that one cause of religious experience may lie in a conviction of the objectivity of moral values.

A sense of dependence, of lack of self-sufficiency, is another possible origin. It may, perhaps, not be the ultimate one, but a kind of step on the way, itself induced by something more primary.

We end, as we began, with Freud. Religious experience may spring from 'wishful thinking'. This is a reasonable interpretation, as applied to religious experience, of some of Freud's suggestions, already referred to in Chapter 2 and to be discussed more fully in Chapter 11, about the origins of religious belief. It would be so nice if there were a Heavenly Father to whom we could turn in time of trouble, a Father who never lets us down, an all-powerful Father with a beneficent plan for the whole universe. Is it not odd, asks Freud, that the beliefs of the religious man are so much in accordance with what we should like to be the case? Isn't there a catch somewhere? Ought we not to be suspicious of people who believe that the world functions in ways clearly to their advantage? Is it not likely that they believe what they do because they want to believe it, not because there is any real evidence for it? Elaborating on this, we may suggest: Is it not the case that religious experiences are self-induced (but not consciously) in the religious believer, who wants the experience of having communications from his God, and so, not surprisingly, finds he has such communications?

I do not claim that this list of origins of religious experience is either exhaustive or exclusive. But it is long enough not to need adding to further, and it contains a sufficient variety of cases.

Where there are so many possibilities of accounting for religious experiences in terms of natural causes the impulse towards accounting for them in terms of supernatural (in particular, divine) causes is bound to be weakened. At the same time, it must be stressed again that not one of these suggested natural causes can plausibly be presented as the sole cause of all religious experiences. Perhaps each covers a part of the field; but there can be no certainty that, taken together, they all cover the whole field. Nothing that has so far been said rules out the possibility of a divine cause of certain experiences not accounted for, or not sufficiently well accounted for, by the natural causes mentioned; or for that matter, many might say, of a divine cause as an ultimate cause of all religious experiences, which lies behind and works through more proximate natural causes, though we shall have occasion subsequently to limit this latter suggestion.

The third of the four questions with which I began was: How can we tell a genuine from a non-genuine religious experience? Clearly, no one can claim to have had a religious experience unless he is fairly certain how to distinguish a genuine case of religious experience from something that is merely masquerading as religious experience. It would be a good thing if the criteria to which the experient appeals were public criteria—criteria that the outsider can also apply—but this is not absolutely necessary. Still, it is desirable, and in the absence of agreed public criteria of genuineness, claims to have had a religious experience are likely to meet with respect, perhaps, but a withholding of acceptance.

We need, to begin with, to settle what we are to mean by a genuine religious experience. I discussed the concept of religious experience fairly fully earlier in this chapter, and we noted there that there is some ambiguity in this expression. If we are to raise the question, 'How do we know when something is a genuine religious experience?' with much hope of success, some at least of this ambiguity will have to be dispelled.

Let us, then, lay it down that by 'genuine religious experience' we mean: 'an experience not merely self-induced, or induced by any other finite cause or causes alone, but induced by God, and one that is an experience of communication of God with the experient'. I say 'merely self-induced' rather than 'self-induced' because I do not wish to preclude by definition the possibility of someone's arguing that conviction of sin—which might be self-induced—is a necessary, even if not a sufficient, condition of having a religious experience. As I have earlier said, I do not wish to argue in this way myself, but I am prepared to acknowledge that it is a line which it is perfectly possible to take.

I do not claim that the definition just given is the only one by which we might define 'genuine religious experience', and I do not wish to deny that there are difficulties about this definition as it stands. I think nevertheless that the definition I have given is likely to meet with fairly general acceptance from religious believers; and I hope that it is neither so wide nor so minimal as not to give us anything worth arguing about.

Now we may embark on the discussion of the question, 'How can we distinguish a genuine religious experience from a non-genuine one?'. The obvious places to look for an answer are three in number: to the origins of the alleged religious experience, to some feature of the experience itself, or to its consequences. Let us consider these in turn.

Can we tell a genuine from a non-genuine religious experience by considering its natural origins or presumed origins? I am in two minds about this. One half of me rejects this suggestion at once. There seems no reason why of two alleged religious experiences having apparently the same natural origin one may not be judged genuine and the other not. In general, of no one origin or group of origins can it be said that it is necessary if religious experience is to take place; in other words, of no one origin or group of origins can it be said that it is necessary to the genuineness of religious experience. Whatever its supposed origins, a given alleged religious experience might be genuine (or non-genuine, as the case may be). Its genuineness or non-genuineness must be established by a consideration of something other than its origins. Some origins may be held to be less irrelevant than others; but I shall not go into this.

Of course, it might be objected that the things I am here thinking of as possible origins of religious experience are all 'natural'. What about supernatural origins? If it could be established that a given religious experience had a supernatural (or, better, a divine) origin would not that entitle us to conclude its genuineness; though only, of course, if 'supernatural origin' is taken to mean 'divine origin'? (This is why, incidentally, in the previous section, I contrasted 'natural' and 'divine', rather than 'natural' and 'supernatural'. This point is worth making; I think that sometimes it is obscured in discussion of the subject. People who talk about 'a supernatural realm' talk about other occupants of it than God; and, in general, talk about the supernatural need not be religious talk.) However, how is a divine origin to be established? This is precisely the point at issue. On the definition of 'religious experience' that we have adopted, to say that if it could be established that an experience purporting to be a communication from God had a divine origin then it could be accepted as genuine is to say no more than that if the experience could be established as genuine then it could be accepted as genuine. This hardly advances the investigation.

On the one hand, then, I want to say that natural origins can be ruled out when we are considering the question of criteria for whether alleged religious experiences are genuine or not.

On the other hand, I am not so sure. Suppose one were convinced by, say, the Freudian view that religion can be accounted for in terms of wish-fulfilment. Should this not lead to a conviction that at least some religious experiences are not genuine, because merely self-induced? Suppose the Freudian story is thought to be fairly plausible as applied to at least some people. And suppose now that other origin stories are thought to be plausible as applied to other people. Would it not then be natural to say that people's claims to religious experience were likely to be mistaken; that at any rate a large number of alleged religious experiences were not genuine? There is a great deal of supposition here, but that does not matter. I have earlier cast doubt on whether any of the origin stories I have considered is capable of being established with certainty. In the present context the very real difficulty that exists in establishing the truth of these accounts is not relevant. It is enough that we should be prepared to *suppose* them, by some means or other, shown to possess some degree of likelihood. The question is whether, supposing these accounts were accepted, we should be prepared in the light of this to say of even some, however few, claims to religious experience that they were not genuine. If the answer is yes, then it seems that, after all, origins must be sometimes relevant to the question of the genuineness of religious experiences. It should perhaps be said here that although, as I remarked earlier, a single experience might sometimes be accounted for in terms both of a natural and of a divine origin— 'God works through natural causes'—it is in practice true that a plausible account in terms of natural causes tends to render an account in terms of a divine cause otiose. More particularly, a plausible account in terms of natural causes of a kind which implied that the experiences in question could be completely accounted for in terms of self-inducement would be actually incompatible with an account of them in terms of a divine cause.

A reconciliation between the opposing points of view may perhaps be found thus. An appeal to natural origins if taken alone cannot settle doubts about the genuineness of claims to religious experience, except, of course, in the case just referred to. Generally speaking, a genuine and a non-genuine experience may have the same natural origin. But this does not rule out the appeal to natural origins as entirely irrelevant. If on other grounds we think we have reason to suspect the genuineness of a given claim, an appeal to origins may be made in support of this suspicion. In fact, the difficulty of uncovering the origins of religious experiences is partly overcome by this. If we think we have reason on other grounds to doubt the genuineness of an alleged religious experience this may lead us to look for a natural origin for it; and we will be the more easily satisfied that we have established a natural origin because we have begun on the assumption that the experience is not genuine. Indeed, I suspect that, in general, a belief that it has such-and-such an origin is seldom our first reason for doubting the genuineness of an alleged religious experience. It is more likely to be something about its content, or about its effect, or lack of effect, on the life of the person who has had it, that sows the seeds of doubt.

One other point needs to be made before I leave the question whether an appeal to their origins may determine the genuineness of alleged religious experiences. On the definition which I have adopted, an experience that was not genuinely but only apparently religious might, among other things, be one that was merely self-induced. The notion of 'self-inducement' can give rise to difficulty. On the Freudian view, a religious experience (that is, what religious people would call a religious experience) might, and indeed probably would, be self-induced *unconsciously*. In such a case, and this is like so many things in Freud, it is difficult to see what empirical tests could be applied to establish whether a given experience was self-induced. The experient certainly would not know. A psychologist investigating him might satisfy himself on the matter, but he would probably do so because he was operating with a particular rather complex theory of the unconscious and its workings which might itself be rejected by others. Does this mean that an explanation in terms of mere self-inducement is precisely on a level with an explanation in terms of God-inducement? In a sense, this is so. Clear, indubitable, empirical demonstration is impossible in either case. I should myself want to claim that the 'mere self-inducement' type of explanation nevertheless has greater force than the God-inducement type and where available is to be preferred. I should claim this on the basis of the general principle that where an explanation in terms of some natural activity can be found—and whatever its difficulties the self-inducement explanation is at least that—one should prefer it to an explanation in terms of supernatural activity; though I should not wish to claim that this principle is itself conclusively demonstrable to someone who is not disposed to accept it.

I have considered the view that the criterion of genuineness in religious experiences may lie in their origins. This, it will be remembered, was only one of three possibilities. The second view to be examined is that which holds that there is some feature of a religious experience itself which guarantees its genuineness. It is the view that religious experiences bear the marks of their authenticity upon their own faces.

This will not do. Someone who has himself not had anything that he is prepared to say was a genuine religious experience (though he may have had experiences that he thinks are probably like those that other people describe as religious experiences) is not going to be helped in his difficulty by being told that if his experiences were genuine he would just know—perhaps, just feel—them to be so. This is the very thing that he does not know, and what he wants is guidance on what feature or features in the experience he is to take note of. There is no such feature as the feature of 'being genuine' as an immediately graspable thing. It is misleading to speak as if there were such a feature. It suggests that reasons are being given for a claim for which in fact no reasons are being given at all. 'This experience is a genuine religious experience because it possesses a certain special feature, a feature possessed by all genuine religious experiences and by nothing that is not a genuine religious experience, but that is not susceptible of definition and must be immediately recognized.' To say that, looks as if one were saying, 'This experience is a genuine religious experience *because* . . .' (giving a reason); whereas, in fact, it says no more than does, 'This is a genuine religious experience'; and the question, 'How do you *know*?' remains unanswered. A method of discriminating between genuine and non-genuine that consists merely in seeing that X is genuine while Y is not, is not a method of discrimination at all. It is not just that it is of no help to the outsider, though this is obviously so. It is of no help even to the experient himself. Just to feel that something is the case, just to have an intuition that matters are so-and-so, is not to have a reason. A wise man does not trust to his intuitions alone, but looks around for reasons to back them up. Without reasons he is in no better a position than the man who is in doubt and lacks even intuition. ('By intuition' is a possible answer to a question about how someone came as a matter of fact to believe something. It is not a possible answer to a question about how he can establish the validity of his belief.) The intuitionist as much as anyone else must be able to distinguish the specific features of an experience that make him say of it that it is genuine.

Of course, intuition has its place. But certainly the present method will not do alone, any more than would the consideration of origins. In combination with each other and with the third method, to which we now turn, they may be worth a great deal more than any one of them is worth alone.

We must now consider whether their results may provide the test for genuineness in religious experiences. William James made a good deal of this, giving a lengthy account of the fruits of religious experience in his chapters on 'Saintliness' (James, pp. 271–325). Others would reject results in favour of the notion we have just discussed, that of self-authenticity. James is surely on the stronger ground. Though the results of religious experience need not be public, they are likely to be—saintliness is something you can verify by observation—and some sort of public test is desirable, if it can be found. On the other hand, may we not want to say that a person's life could exhibit such-and-such a change of direction, or such-and-such features of the kind James means by saintliness, and yet that this might have followed upon an experience that the person was mistaken in thinking a religious one? That is, do we not want to preserve a use for the expression 'genuine religious experience' apart from any consideration of the results of alleged religious experiences? Is it self-contradictory to say of someone: 'He had a genuine religious experience, but his subsequent life exhibited none of the marks of saintliness'? I am not sure what the answer to this is. Certainly, it seems to make sense to say of a religious experience that it was genuine but without lasting effects. Is the appeal to results really only a way of testing for religious experiences with relatively permanent effects? I am not certain what is the answer to this question.

I have not considered that it is any part of my task to remove entirely the ambiguity which surrounds the term 'religious experience'. I have indicated broadly how I myself prefer to use the term, but I do not wish to rule out other uses as mistaken. None, indeed, is mistaken; though some—especially the tendency to use it so as to exclude the Public Experience View—are in various ways unwise. While a measure of ambiguity is allowed to remain, the question of the validity of religious experience, or, as I have been considering it here, the question of its criteria of genuineness, cannot be finally answered.

Nevertheless, it seems right to say that the third of the possible criteria I have been examining—that of results—is the most promising. It is a public criterion, and that is a good thing. So, too, of course, is the origin criterion, but that one, as we saw, raises other difficulties. It is probably easier to get agreement on the results of a religious experience than on its origins. I do not mean that it is in itself easy, but only that it is easier. For one thing, the marks of the saintly life are fairly readily listed and discoverable; and, for another, given that a certain experience has taken place, it is easier to follow it into the future as its effects successively show themselves than to search back into events that are now over and completed for problematic causes. The results criterion is public and practical. Further, it is, I think, the criterion that people generally do in fact apply in this matter. If they were told that someone had had a remarkable religious experience, it would, I think, strike most people as proper to retort (if they thought they had reason to): 'That was no genuine religious experience; he is as drunken and dishonest as ever he was'. A reply in terms of one's beliefs about the origins of his experience would be relevant, too, of course, but probably harder to make with any claim to certainty. I suspect that whereas some people might claim that an origin in, say, drug-taking was not necessarily incompatible with being a genuine religious experience, fewer would think this about a failure to have any outward effects in the sense of 'changing a man's life'.

These are generalizations, of course, and there are bound to be exceptions. There may be cases where it is comparatively easy to agree on the origins of a certain ostensible religious experience and very difficult to agree on what precisely are its results. This is, indeed, in many ways a matter of making the best of a bad job. The results criterion is not without its faults, as I have already indicated. It is not the case that it clearly passes a test which the other two as clearly fail. It would be truer to say that all fail. Certainly each of them fails if it is put forward as the sole criterion. But some criterion we must have; or, at least, the man who claims to have religious experiences must have a criterion. For, as I insisted earlier, such a claim is pointless unless the person making it is able to say, if only to himself, in what way he could tell a genuine religious experience from something that was not. Unless he can do this, the claim to have religious experience will mean nothing even to him (and if he thinks it does, he is deceiving himself), let alone to anybody else. Some criterion there must be; and, in a sense, the bill will be met by arbitrarily laying one down. But it is clearly more satisfactory if a criterion can be decided upon by examining those that people have considered themselves to have some justification for adopting, and choosing from among them. This I have done, and the results criterion is the one that I offer. It is the least objectionable. The others must still be allowed a place; but preferably, I think, only as auxiliaries to it.

All that has been said so far in this chapter, though important in its own right, is preliminary to the last of the four questions I mentioned at the beginning. 'Is it possible to infer the existence of God from the fact, if it is a fact, that people have religious experiences?' We can immediately simplify matters by disposing of the implied doubt of the phrase 'if it is a fact'. It is certainly a fact that people claim to have religious experiences; and let us assume, for the sake of argument, that they have good reasons for this claim. Of course, they may be mistaken. Our discussion has brought out how difficult it is to find a satisfactory way of determining when people are or are not mistaken about this. It is not, of course, logically impossible that people are always mistaken when they claim religious experience; that is, that the experiences they have (for it cannot be doubted that people do have 'experiences': what is at issue is how these are to be described) are never, in the sense defined earlier, genuinely religious. However, I do not propose for present purposes to question the fact that people do have experiences of a kind that would be called 'religious'.

The mere having of these experiences, it is clear, is not the end of the matter. There is no particular virtue in merely being in such-and-such a psychological state (I am assuming the Private

Experience View). The value of religious experience to the believer lies in the deeper acquaintance with God which it may be assumed by him to give, or in the way in which it brings home to him shortcomings in his life, etc. As far as the discovery of a rational basis for religion is concerned, its value lies in the evidence which it is held to provide for the existence of God.

Does it provide good evidence? It must be said that it certainly does not provide evidence that the non-believer might be convinced by. The case is otherwise if we look at it from the point of view of the man who believes in God already; and in this respect, as might have been expected, it is in the same position as the other theistic proofs we have been examining. But from the point of view of the non-believer it has the obvious practical drawback that what is offered as evidence here is private and not public. The other theistic proofs, whatever their shortcomings in other respects, are at least based on evidence which, if it is evidence at all, is nearer to being 'public' evidence: order in the universe, the idea of God, the existence of finite things. Before the Argument from Religious Experience can get started, we must be persuaded that those who claim religious experience are not deceiving either others or themselves; and, as we have seen, this is not easy to do.

The objection to the Argument from Religious Experience that I want to stress is more serious than this. I have earlier hinted at this objection, but I can now make it explicitly.

We can most easily see the difficulty I have in mind if we approach it through an analogous case previously referred to— that of our knowledge of other persons. Whether this in fact is an analogous case might be disputed; but I do not wish to embark on a discussion of this point. Now it would be logically absurd to claim that you could prove the existence of other persons *from your own reactions to them alone*. 'Reactions to other persons' would normally be so used as to imply 'Other persons exist'. Unless persons exist there can obviously be no reactions to them. This means that to attempt to prove the existence of a person from one's own 'reactions' alone would obviously be to beg the question. In the case of knowledge of other persons, no one is likely ever to want to make this claim. Yet in the case of knowledge of God this is just what, on the Private Experience View, the Argument from Religious Experience involves. From the fact that some people have had experiences which they believe—rightly, we may concede for present purposes—to be experiences of God, it is possible to conclude that God exists: so the argument may be supposed to run. Such an argument could never stand on its own feet as the only source of knowledge of God's existence. If the experiences are experiences of God—reactions to God, to use the terminology we employed in the analogous case—then, of course, God's existence may be said to follow from the fact of the experiences; in the sense that they could not be experiences *of God* unless God did exist. It is clear that this is no argument to the existence of God. It is a statement of the obvious.

Suppose the advocate of the Argument from Religious Experience now admits that it is begging the question to pretend to argue to the existence of God from experiences of God. Suppose he now says that he will express his argument as one simply from certain psychological states, not now defined to include reference to God. What then? He is on no stronger ground. Nothing of present relevance follows from the fact that someone is in a certain psychological state. Nothing, that is, follows about the existence of any being other than the person himself who is enjoying that state.

In short, if religious experiences are so defined as to contain no necessary reference to God, nothing can follow, from the mere fact that religious experiences occur, that bears upon the question whether God, or anything else, except perhaps the experient, exists. But the religious believer does commonly want to define 'religious experience' so that it is synonymous with 'experience of God'. In this case, however, to argue that because religious experiences occur God must exist is to beg the question, and is no argument at all.

There can be no doubt that religious experiences, if these are experiences of God, do in a sense entail the existence of God—in the sense, already referred to, that you cannot have an experience of, or a reaction to, X, unless X exists to be experienced or reacted to. This cannot of itself constitute a proof of the existence of X. The existence of X, and the question whether a certain experience is an experience of X, being logically connected, stand or fall together. If we know, or think we know, on other grounds, that X exists, we may try to settle the question whether we have, unquestionably, 'experiences' of X. What we cannot do is what the Argument from Religious Experience does, that is, start from the experiences themselves and then 'argue' to the divine cause that has already been provided by understanding (it may be implicitly) 'religious experience' as 'experience *of God*'. This is to define God into existence, and that kind of existence is not worth having.

Two points need to be made in conclusion. First, it is worth stressing yet again the lesson that has emerged consistently from our discussion of the theistic proofs. If these arguments are interpreted as attempts to prove God 'objectively', to a supposed open-minded man without bias either way in the matter of religious belief—and even more to the sceptic—they fail. You cannot argue to God in a religious vacuum, or in a hostile environment. The present argument will work, for the man who believes in God already, as a help to the clarification of his ideas of God. As a method of showing the existence of a God not otherwise known or believed to exist the Argument from Religious Experience is indeed absurd. It is not absurd if considered as a method of getting to know something about a God already known, or believed, to exist. The case of knowledge of other persons is again helpful. It is logically absurd to suppose that one's only ground, or one's first reason, for knowing that someone exists might be one's own reactions to him. One could not speak of having reactions to him unless one already believed him to exist. Nevertheless, this is, in fact, one of the ways in which we learn things about people whom, on other grounds, we do know already to exist.

Secondly, it is important to realize that the strictures that I have passed on the Argument from Religious Experience are directed against the way in which it is normally presented—that is, in a way which assumes the Private Experience View. But on the Public Experience View a version of the argument might be developed which escapes much of the criticism I have levelled against it here. It is instructive to compare with the usual present-day understanding and use of 'religious experience' the views of some of the great mystics in the history of the Christian Church. Writers like Saint Teresa, or the anonymous author of that marvellous English mystical classic, *The Cloud of Unknowing*, assume belief in God on the part of the reader, and there is no suggestion of any deep interest in psychological states for their own sake (they are a means to an end), and certainly no suggestion that the existence of God might be proved from a consideration of psychological states. The author of *The Cloud* spends a good deal of time on practical questions about the mechanics of prayer, and in general of how to live the life of contemplation. The questions with which he is concerned are more often than not questions about what I am calling Public Experience; questions about the precise way in which the believer with a bent for contemplation should immerse himself in practices that will help towards the attainment of the ultimate end of contemplation— union with God. For such a person conviction of the existence of God will become stronger through such practices, and his knowledge of God's nature deeper: such at least is the intention, and there can be little doubt that on the whole the practice of contemplation does attain this end. Submission to the authority and tradition of the Church is at all times presupposed. What the practices are claimed to provide is not belief itself, but deeper insight into what is believed already. This is an interpretation of 'religious experience'—not that this phrase itself would have been used by Saint Teresa or the author of *The Cloud*—that treats it altogether more fruitfully than does the usual present-day Private Experience View.

CHAPTER 9

The Problem of Evil

THIS is a suitable point at which to pause for stocktaking. After the discussion of preliminary or general questions in the first three chapters, we embarked directly upon a consideration of the place of reason in religion. The traditional view on this matter is that religion has a rational basis, in the shape principally of the three standard arguments for the existence of God, the Ontological Argument, the Cosmological Argument, and the Argument from Design; and we examined these arguments fairly closely in the ensuing chapters. We then moved on to consider two further theistic arguments of a less traditional character—the Moral Argument and the Argument from Religious Experience; in both cases combining with our examination of the arguments a discussion of wider themes, themselves of considerable importance in the philosophy of religion: the general question of the relation between religion and morality, the religious philosophy of Kant, the nature of religious experience and the question of the criteria of genuineness in religious experience.

All this has taken us a fair distance along the road we set ourselves to travel, that is, to treat the question of the place of reason in religion as our central theme while at the same time considering other topics in the philosophy of religion as these suggested themselves.

It is not possible to state a single, simple conclusion to the foregoing chapters. Certainly, to say unqualifiedly that religion has *no* rational basis, on the ground that the theistic 'proofs' have logical flaws, would be misleading. I have been at pains to approach these arguments from the point of view of the *intentions*

125

of those who have in the past offered them, and I have suggested respects in which, despite their logical shortcomings, they are nevertheless of value.

The time has come for a change of direction. We have examined what has most commonly been thought to be involved in the claim that religion is rational. Let us now turn to consider some of the forms that are taken by the view that religion is not rational.

The chief obstacle in the way of religious belief has probably always been the so-called problem of evil. This is very much a practical problem as it affects the ordinary man who may be compelled to stand by helpless and watch his wife or child dying in agony from some incurable disease. It is also a theoretical problem. The case for the irrationality of religion has found powerful support in the problem of evil, which seems to show up a fundamental inconsistency in the religious position.

The problem is often put in the form of a dilemma, as follows. God, religious people believe, is both all-good and all-powerful. But there is evil and pain in the world. Now, either God causes, or at least permits, this evil or he does not. So God is either not all-good or not all-powerful.

If this dilemma is accepted, the consequences for religion seem serious—serious, that is, for anyone who may wish to maintain the rationality of religion. It seems that there is a contradiction in the religious conception of God. He is claimed to possess two attributes which, taken together, are in conflict, or so it seems, with plain observed fact. One or the other ought surely to be dropped in the interests of consistency. Yet dare the Christian drop either? Would not this constitute abandoning essential parts of the Christian faith?

Paradoxically, the existence of pain has led to belief in God as well as denial of him. For instance, C. E. M. Joad, the author of many books on philosophy, as a young man rejected belief in God because such belief seemed to him impossible to maintain in the face of the existence of evil. In later life he became a Christian largely as a result of the train of thought started in his mind by his own serious illness and pain. It is, indeed, often claimed by Christians, and with justice, that personal suffering leading as it may to a realization of one's own lack of self-sufficiency, can actually have the effect of inducing or strengthening belief in God rather than of destroying it. Kant's Moral Argument for the existence of God might be interpreted as yet another illustration of this process. (Because there is so much undeserved suffering in this world there must be a God who will redress the balance in another.) Evil works both ways. Pain has its uses, as we shall again have occasion to note later.

This, however, does not dispose of the problem of evil. For if there were only a single instance of apparently undeserved, apparently inexplicable pain, the problem would still be there, as much as if there were millions of such instances. Attempts to solve the problem of evil do, indeed, generally take the form of attempts to minimize it, as if in the hope that by limiting its extent one might in the end make it vanish away. But, to the believer in God, the problem is exactly as great however narrow or wide may be the extent of evil. There is as much difficulty in reconciling the belief that God is good with the existence of a single case of evil as there is in reconciling it with a thousand cases.

The problem of evil exists for the religious believer in a way that it does not for the atheist. The man who does not believe in a good God anyway is not faced with the difficulty of reconciling belief in a good God with the facts of evil. It is much less likely to occur to him to approach evil and suffering with the question, 'What is it for?', or 'What is the meaning of it all?'. He may, of course, find such questions coming into his mind; but if they do he is likely to settle on an answer satisfactory to himself without too much trouble. Questions like this occur much more naturally to the religious man—not surprisingly, for a large part of what is involved in being religious is precisely that one is disposed to look for an explanation of the existence of things at all and of why they are as they are. It is the combination of this natural inclination in the religious man with the beliefs about God of the Christian religious tradition, that creates the problem.

It is a problem that Christian theologians have always been aware of, and one that they have always been willing to attempt to answer. As I remarked at the beginning of the chapter, this is

probably the chief obstacle in the way of religious belief, and
Christian apologists have been sensible of this; although there is
a tendency in some sceptical writers to present the problem as if
they had thought of it themselves for the first time in history and
were laying it before the theologian with the challenge: 'There!
Try to answer that!'. Of course, although answers exist, we may
well be forced to decide that they are not satisfactory: this we
must see.

There is a fundamental distinction that needs now to be made.
I have been writing indiscriminately of the problem of 'evil',
of 'pain', of 'suffering'. It is usual, however, in systematic
discussions of this theme, to make a distinction between two
different aspects of the problem, or, it may be, a distinction
between two different but related problems. This is the distinction sometimes expressed as that between 'moral evil' and 'natural
evil', sometimes as that between the problem of sin (or of evil,
where the term is used in a narrower sense) and the problem of
pain or suffering. The former way of making the distinction,
though usefully simple, has the disadvantage that it appears to
beg an important question—that of the relation between sin and
moral wrongdoing. I shall, accordingly, adopt the latter way, and
state the distinction as one between the problem of sin and the
problem of pain. The problem of pain is, of course, the problem
created for the religious believer by the existence of that kind of
pain and suffering that is the result of natural calamities, or of
disease in so far as this is thought of as not the effect of human
will. The problem of sin is the problem created by the existence of
that kind of evil which may be interpreted as springing from the
characters or wills of men—war, acts of cruelty, even famine
(in so far as this may be sometimes seen as the result of man's
selfishness). The distinction between the two kinds of problem
is not as sharp as has sometimes been supposed, and I have some
sympathy with the attempts that have been made to consider
them as no more than aspects of a single problem admitting of a
single solution. In what follows I shall work on the assumption
that there are two distinct problems here; but it is only right to
say that there may well be borderline cases that we cannot with
confidence assign to one of these headings to the exclusion of the

other, and that there are probably events that will not fit easily under *either* of these headings as they are generally understood.

Let us begin with the problem of pain. It is perhaps hardly necessary to elaborate on the facts. Everyone has some personal experience of pain. Much pain, it is true, is relatively trivial; but there is also pain that is far from trivial.

There is the pain suffered by animals ('Nature, red in tooth and claw'), and in the case of the higher animals at least there is no need glibly to suppose, as there seems reason to suppose in the case of more primitive organisms, that the animals in question 'do not *really* feel pain—not as we feel pain'. Some writers have laid stress on the 'suffering and frustration' involved in the evolutionary process. This is, of course, to put the matter an-thropomorphically; and there is not necessarily great pain in company with the workings of natural selection. The anthropo-morphic character of most people's attitude to animals is of some importance here. To put it over-strongly, the significance of animal suffering perhaps lies less in the facts, such as they are, of suffering, than in the interpretation put upon them by the human onlooker. Even if—which is wildly unlikely—there is nothing in the animal kingdom at all closely resembling human experience of pain, it remains true that many men think there is, and we are not in a position to say with certainty that they are wrong in so thinking. Indeed, so long as humane men consider that at least certain animals suffer a degree of pain above what we might agree in supposing trivial, the problem will remain. After all, it is not the animals themselves who are exercised about the problem of pain. They have the pain, but not the problem. It is men for whom the problem of pain exists, and as long as men think of animals as they do (we need not attempt to settle whether they are right in so thinking) there will be a problem of pain generated for the Christian when he observes the animal life around him and reflects upon its history and present condition. All this is not, of course, meant in the least to imply that the problem is unreal. To say that it arises less from the facts, what-ever they may be, than from the interpretation put upon them by men, is not to say that the problem is merely invented and not discovered. It is real enough. But it does to some extent depend upon human decision, or perhaps merely human habit, on the question of what is the best way of describing what goes on in the animal world. To a mechanist, preferring, as he does, so to classify animals, and probably human beings as well, as to bring out their affinities with machines, there would probably be no problem of pain. On the whole, the Christian is not likely to be a mechanist (though it is not ruled out that he can be: Descartes was, with regard to animals). The problem of pain, so far as the evidence from the animal world is concerned, arises chiefly for those who regard animals anthropomorphically. This way of regarding them is neither right nor wrong. It is merely one of the basic ways in which men do regard animals. In this sense it is the case, as I have said, that the problem of pain, as far as it is supposed to arise from a consideration of the animal kingdom, depends to a considerable extent upon the way the facts are interpreted, and would probably not arise at all if these facts were, as they can be, interpreted differently.

In any case, it is human rather than animal pain—possibly analogous, possibly not—that men have chiefly in mind in discussing this subject. One respect in which human pain seems to differ from that of lower animals is in the extent to which human pain is often 'mental' rather than 'physical'. This is in some ways a misleading pair of terms with which to point the distinction, but it is a convenient one. Human beings, people suppose, when they suffer mental anguish, from whatever cause, are experiencing something that animals, even the higher animals, never experience; or, if they do experience it, what they experience is only the palest of copies, the merest glimpse from the threshold. People sometimes arrange human beings in a hierarchy of 'sensitiveness', according to the degree of mental torment they are liable to suffer. It is even sometimes suggested that it is on mental anguish that the 'real' problem of pain centres; that physical suffering is not sufficiently human to set the problem sharply, is too close to the merely organic or even 'animal' side of man and not close enough to the 'soul' or the 'spiritual', and hence religiously important, side; that a mother's grief over her child's painful death poses the problem in a way that the child's suffering itself does not. This tendency to play down the importance of 'merely physical' pain seems to me mistaken. For one thing, it is to put a totally irrelevant premium upon certain kinds of temperament, and upon certain accidents of circumstance. At the same time, I am not impressed by attempts to lay the emphasis in the opposite direction, as in a suggestion that has been made that mental anguish ought not to present any problem to the Christian, for Christ is supposed to have overcome it, so that it is physical pain that Christians ought to be puzzled by. I see no value in attempts to exalt 'physical' over 'mental', or 'mental' over 'physical'.

I mentioned above that attempts to solve the problem of pain generally take the form of attempts to minimize it. We have just seen this process at work. Physical and mental pain together may be said to constitute, in a purely arithmetical sense, a greater problem than either of them taken alone; so if one can be eliminated the problem is immediately halved. This curious kind of reasoning is reflected also in the distinction between human and animal pain with which we were concerned. This distinction is sometimes drawn as a preliminary to the setting aside of animal pain, on the grounds, already referred to, that we cannot be sure that animals feel pain as we do and so we had better not complicate things by considering them as well as humans. This line of reasoning is to be found, once again, in the argument sometimes met with that the part of the universe capable of suffering pain—sentient and self-conscious organisms—is infinitesimal in relation to the universe as a whole.

One of the most interesting of these minimizing arguments is that of C. S. Lewis, in his *The Problem of Pain*, that 'there is no such thing as a sum of suffering, for no one suffers it'. That is to say, there cannot be more suffering in the universe than the greatest amount that a single individual can experience. It is pointless to add together the pains of different individuals; for no one in fact suffers that. If there were only three organisms in the universe capable of suffering pain, call them A, B, and C, and all were actually in pain, B to a greater degree (assuming that we had some way of measuring and comparing the amount of pain suffered by different individuals) than either A or C, then the greatest pain existing in the universe would be B's pain, not A's pain + B's pain + C's pain. Pains exist as they are experienced by organisms, and it makes no sense to talk as if they could be isolated from the organisms that are experiencing them and all heaped up together to make one immense pain. A pain that is not somebody's pain (that is, the pain of some individual; for you cannot feel my pain, and I cannot feel yours) is not a pain at all.

This argument is both neat and true. There is, *in this sense*, no such thing as a sum of suffering. The fact remains, however, that there are a great many people who are in pain; and to point out to X that he cannot have Y's and Z's pains as well as his own is cold comfort to him who probably thinks anyway that he is suffering as no man ever suffered before. There is a kind of Parkinson's Law of pain: pain expands to fill the available capacity for it. It is possible to distinguish trivial pains from serious ones and serious ones from very serious ones; but there comes a point where differences of degree become unimportant, and as far as the patient is concerned the pain spreads out to occupy all the available metaphorical space. (The childless housewife with a maid considers herself busy, and really is. The mother with four small children and no help also considers herself busy, and really is. The former may be as overworked and harassed as the latter, and for an outsider to say smugly that she ought not to be is no help to her. She cannot imagine how she could fit anything else in, because she has no first-hand experience of having to do it; just as the mother, in the days when she had only one child, herself could not imagine how women managed when they had two or even (Good heavens!) three. We are all as busy as can be; but a Supreme Being must look with amusement at what busy-ness means to some of us.) True, the greatest amount of pain that can exist is the greatest amount that one individual can suffer. But in the matter of pain each individual is judge in his own case; and the number of individuals each of whom may consider himself to be suffering the greatest amount of pain of which he is capable is large. Although indeed X may not also suffer Y's or Z's pain, or they his, a world where X, Y, and Z are all severally suffering may in a perfectly intelligible sense, though not C. S. Lewis's, be said to contain more pain than one in which only X is suffering.

Pain has the useful function of giving warning of illness, and this fact is sometimes appealed to as a way of solving—again by minimizing—the problem of pain. But this is hardly to the point. It is not pain considered as offering warning of disease or danger that gives rise to the problem. For what of pain that goes on after its warning has been heeded? What of the disease itself of which it is a warning? Related to this is the other function of pain, previously mentioned, that of bringing a man up short and showing him his own insufficiency, of shocking him out of complacency and impressing upon him that he is not after all the master of his fate and captain of his soul—its function of 'bringing a man to God'. Here, again, we may say that it is not in respect of this function that the problem is likely to arise. What of those who escape suffering and go on being complacent? What of those who get a great deal more pain than they need to 'bring them to God'? What of the innocent and already religiously-inclined who suffer, it seems, so undeservedly? Why, in short, is pain so apparently unfairly distributed? What of those who react to pain not by being brought round to a confession of dependence on God but by rejecting the God who can use such methods to get what he wants? The problem remains, at least as far as this kind of argument is concerned.

Although none of these attempts to minimize the problem can, taken by itself, be considered to have disposed of it, they do, when added together, constitute a fairly formidable battery. Nevertheless, it remains true, as I said earlier, that the problem cannot be finally disposed of by any method that merely seeks to minimize it —and most of what have been offered as 'solutions' to the problem are in fact, whether or not in intention, no more than this. What is needed—if it can be found—is an approach that will go more nearly to the root of the difficulty.

One way of making such an approach, though it has its own faults of a different kind, may be found if we question something that has been assumed throughout the preceding pages—that is, that it is pain or suffering itself which causes the problem. This we are very apt to think, and with a good deal of justification.

But perhaps too much concentration on people's experiences of pain, or, for that matter, of pleasure, is tantamount to the elevation of symptoms into diseases. After all, in a sense, that people experience pain and pleasure is just a fact about them that in itself creates no particular problem. To a large extent the pains and pleasures we experience are under our own control. Sleep or drugs may put an end to pain for a time; and if a man chooses to take his own life he may put an end to his pain for ever. The problem for the religious believer, it may be said, does not lie in the pain associated with disease and natural calamity but in the very existence of disease and natural calamity, which, even if no one suffered pain through them, would still pose a problem to the would-be believer in an omnipotent, good God.

This view—interestingly developed by Father M. C. D'Arcy in *The Pain of this World and the Providence of God*—is ingenious, but it will hardly do. Perhaps we do tend to exalt our feelings of pleasure and pain too much, and perhaps there are more important things than these; but pleasure and pain do nevertheless make up an essential part of human life. It may be the case that the belief that God wills man's happiness is not to be identified with the belief that God wills for man absence from pain; but it is hard to suppose that the undoubted existence of extreme pain does not tell against the former belief. No doctrine of pain as merely negative—as privation of good rather than as something positive in itself—can satisfy the man who is here and now going through the very positive experience of suffering pain. It is difficult to believe that if pain did not exist at all—no physical pain, no mental anguish of grief, etc.—the fact that there is disease (supposing even that in those circumstances we should have the concept of disease at all), and that there are earthquakes, famines, fatal flashes of lightning, etc., would of themselves have seemed to set a problem to the religious believer—unless, of course, he wanted to find a cause of quarrel with God in the fact that we are not immortal. It is not disease and death of themselves that set the problem so much as the suffering that accompanies them. (I do not, of course, deny that, for example, premature death or insanity can be called evils in themselves, distinct from the suffering that may accompany them. But I do not think they would be likely to strike people as evils if they were never so accompanied.) At the same time, to be fair to Father D'Arcy, it is only right to say that in the book mentioned—which, in any case, is written in dialogue form, with the author making no contribution of importance in his own voice—the two problems of pain and sin are considered together, and a single solution sought for both; and from this point of view the suggestion that pain is not as important as sometimes supposed seems not without plausibility, because pain is seen always in connexion with something that is, to the Christian, much more serious, namely, sin.

Must we now conclude that there is no solution to the Christian's problem of pain? There remains one other possible line of thought on the matter—which has also, as it happens, been developed by Father D'Arcy, though it is to be found in some form or other in the work of many other writers. This is the argument that good is somehow dependent upon evil—in this case, upon suffering; that, for instance, character is created by struggling against adversity. This is, of course, true. But much the same objection must be made here as was made in an earlier connexion. This will not satisfactorily account for all suffering; for there is more than enough to bring about this end, and it is the residue, the waste of suffering, that needs to be accounted for.

The conclusion, then, need no longer be delayed. There is no rational solution to the problem of pain—unless it be the solution that the universe was not designed by the Christian God. The Christian, having worked through what suggestions have been offered, and having, as he ought, found them wanting, takes refuge in faith. 'Somehow, though we cannot clearly see how, the existence of suffering in the world is reconcilable with belief in an omnipotent and good God.' Whether this attitude is labelled irrational or rational is perhaps largely a matter of choice.

To some extent, those writers who treat the problem of pain and the problem of sin as aspects of a single problem are right. The clarity that is gained by isolating the component parts of a general problem or family of problems is sometimes illusory. But as long as we know what we are doing there is no great harm in it, and there may well be a gain in our understanding of the separate parts.

That part of the general or overall problem of evil that is known as the problem of sin generally receives a single agreed answer from religious writers, an answer in terms of free will; though it is an answer that tends to generate new problems of its own. The problem itself needs no stating, beyond the mere indication, already given, that it is the problem of how belief in a good, omnipotent God can be reconciled with the existence of that kind of evil in the world that is attributable to the will of man. The solution is to say that God in his omnipotence and benevolence has chosen to create man with the power to choose good or evil, and it follows that man sometimes chooses evil; but the alternative would have been to create not man but something inferior to man—a being without the power of free choice, who would dance to his Master's bidding without, as we say, 'a will of his own'. The existence of sin is part of the price we pay for being what we are; and it is hardly meaningful to suppose that we might have been as we are, yet have inhabited a world without sin.

This solution depends, among other things, upon a particular understanding of the concept of omnipotence—depends, in fact, upon the doctrine that an omnipotent being can exercise his omnipotence in limiting his omnipotence. This is a notion that in itself need present no difficulty. An omnipotent being must have the power to draw limits to his power. The difficulty, however, arises when we consider God's attribute of goodness. If the consequence of God's creating beings with free will, over whose actions he chooses to abandon control, is that those beings proceed to inflict injury on themselves and others, ought not the omnipotent God to throw away the voluntarily assumed snaffle and bit, ought he not to step in and bring the experiment to a close? If he fails to do this, does he deserve to be called all-good? Is not the original dilemma with us still?

Indeed, we may ask, could not God have created beings with free will who yet always chose good and never evil? Such beings would not be us; but they might be sufficiently like us in other respects. Someone might reply that, in that case, there would be no need for the Incarnation and the Atonement, as the orthodox believer interprets them; for these central elements in Christianity would lose their meaning if there were no estrangement between God and man as a result of sin, and there could hardly be this if there were no sin. Under these conditions, indeed, none of the Judaic religions would have been likely to come into existence at all. To create man with free will, in such a way that sin is much more likely than not to follow, and thus (because God, we are told, is good as well as omnipotent) to be put to the necessity of arranging the Incarnation as a way of bringing mankind back from estrangement—all this looks like a divine digging of holes in order to be able to fill them in again. Why did God not exercise greater care and foresight in the first place? He had all the power and all the knowledge needed.

This line of argument may well strike the reader as absurd, and so, of course, to some extent it is. Christians maintain that the language men use of God is analogical language, and not to be taken literally. God, the Christian will say, does not operate in ways that are adequately expressed by the statements of the preceding paragraph. Again, as I have already said, beings of the kind I have described simply would not be *us*; so the whole speculation has for this reason, too, an air of unreality. Nevertheless, the suggestion that men might have been created so that, although they had free will, they always chose the good and refrained from the bad, is a perfectly meaningful one; and, indeed, is no more than a taking to its logical conclusion of a view to be found in some theologians—the view that God may direct that some end may be presented to a man in such a way that he cannot but choose to pursue it. To maintain that a man has free will is—though this is a simplification—to hold that he is able, after rational consideration, to decide to do or not to do a given action; and this is not incompatible either with holding that he always decides the same way or even with holding that his decision is influenced by factors of which he may be unaware. Among those factors there might well be more in the way of divine promptings. God might, for instance, have so arranged things that the good alternative always had an air of attractiveness that the bad lacked. Even if we did not go so far as to require that

God *always* ensured the choice of the good, it would not be unreasonable to suggest that he do so to a greater extent than he seems to. While no doubt not the worst of all possible worlds, this world might well be better than it is. We all feel temptation to do things that may injure others. Sometimes we succumb to temptation and sometimes we do not. It is a perfectly intelligible supposition that we all, while still feeling temptation, might have the 'strength of will' always to resist it. In these circumstances, the world would be a considerably happier and more evil-free place than it is. Of course, the discipline of struggling against temptation might then be less than it is now, and the character-building value of adversity would, no doubt, regretfully have to be bidden farewell; but we would perhaps find an adequate substitute in competition among ourselves in seeing who could outdo the others in good works.

To say it yet again, beings of the kind described would not be men. There is however nothing inherently impossible in God's having created such beings instead of us. The question is whether, if he had, the state of the universe would be preferable to its actual state. More important, would it represent a state of affairs under which the problem of sin would not exist? There can be no doubt that the answer to this latter question is yes.

The dilemma, it seems, remains. The universe being as it is, it seems that there is a conflict involved in believing both that God is omnipotent and that he is benevolent. We need not paint an exaggerated picture of the evil in the world. We may, if we wish, believe it to be very little. But might it not have been less?

Granted the universe as it is, and accepting for the present the traditional way of expressing the matter, the free will solution to the problem of sin has much to be said for it. But are we entirely bound to accept the universe as it is? In a sense, of course, we are so bound, as Carlyle indicated in his reply to Margaret Fuller who had grandly said, 'I accept the universe'—'Gad! she'd better!'. The preceding speculations are theoretical; in practice, we must deal with the world as we find it. They are however sufficient to give grounds for wondering whether the traditional view tells the whole story.

The key concept in the preceding discussion was that of free will. We have had occasion to note in Chapter 7 Kant's grouping of the themes of metaphysics—God, freedom, and immortality. It goes without saying that the first of these themes must occupy a central place in any philosophy of religion; and so perhaps must the third. It may be less obvious that the second deserves a chief place; but it is the case that any philosophy of religion must take seriously the question of the nature of man—if for no other reason than that religion is a human phenomenon—and questions about free will cannot then be avoided.

Controversy about free will goes on in both metaphysics and moral philosophy, and, as often as not, goes on without any reference to religion at all. As traditionally presented, the controversy centres around physical science. This was how Kant himself saw it, as we noted earlier. The traditional warfare has been between Determinists who, inspired by the principle that 'every event has a cause' believe that human decisions can be accounted for in purely causal terms, and, on the other side, Libertarians, who claim for human decisions a special status, beyond the competence of the physicist to explain completely in his own language. This traditional picture has not been changed by the subsequent bringing up on the Determinist side of additional armour in the shape of biological or psychological laws. The Libertarians have generally had fewer arguments on their side, and have limited themselves for the most part to an argument from intuition—an appeal to the consciousness that they claim we have of being free in the moment of decision. (As Dr. Johnson said: 'Sir, We *know* our will is free, and *there's* an end on't'.)

Much of what is commonly said about 'the problem of free will' is open to serious difficulties. For instance, the question whether a man might have decided, or have acted, differently from the way in which he did decide or act, seems to involve the notion of a man as something altogether other than his decisions or actions—perhaps some continuing entity which underlies those decisions and actions. But I am at least to some extent the product of my past decisions and actions. If I today ask whether I could on a certain occasion ten years ago have decided differently, what is the reference of the second 'I' here? This is not the place to pursue these inquiries. I shall content myself with calling attention to the fact that there are difficulties here, and with saying that failure to pursue them further is not meant to indicate contentment with the way in which the controversy has traditionally been carried on.

Kant's own solution to 'the problem of free will' we have noted earlier. In so far as men belong to the 'phenomenal' world they are determined; but through the moral faculty—the practical reason—they are in contact with the 'noumenal' world, where causation does not operate. So man is both determined and free: determined in so far as he is a physical body, free in so far as he is a moral agent.

There was, as we noted, a religious background to Kant's insistence on free will; and, in general, a belief in free will is an important part of the religious view of man. However, support is sometimes offered in the name of religion for the Determinist, not the Libertarian, position. This is done by means of the following argument. Man is in a state of sin—original sin—so that all he does is determined by a fatal flaw in his nature, and although he may want to do good he is impelled irresistibly in the direction of evil. As Ovid said: 'I see and approve better things, but follow worse'. Or St. Paul: 'I find then a law, that, when I would do good, evil is present with me'. This doctrine appears both in relatively extreme and relatively mild versions—phrases like 'total depravity' may or may not be used—but in one form or another it is a doctrine that has been quite widely held. In its extreme forms it is clearly in sharp conflict with the other, and more widely held, Christian belief that man is morally free.

This is not the only argument on the side of Determinism that has been offered in the name of religion. There are also arguments that take as their starting point two of God's attributes, his omniscience and his omnipotence. Let us first consider the former.

It is argued that if God is omniscient, he must know what we shall do on a given future occasion. God cannot know this unless it is already settled, whether *we* know it or not, what we shall do.

So our future actions are determined, and our consciousness of freedom is illusory.

This argument from omniscience is not a strong one. It depends upon the identification of the notions of determination and predictability. It is supposed that if an event can be predicted it must be predetermined. This identification, however, is a mistaken one. If we know people very well—and God may be presumed to know us all a great deal better than any of us knows the others—we can pretty accurately predict what they will do, but we need not suppose that what they do is therefore determined. Saint Augustine long ago disposed of this mistaken identification.

It is perhaps worth noting that it is possible to present the situation without reference to predictability—at least in its normal sense, where prediction is understood to mean prediction of a specific event or set of events to the exclusion of others. Philosophers have called attention to the way in which we tend naturally to think of things as moving through time, as they may move through space, and consequently picture time as a kind of road along which we make our way from birth to death, or perhaps better, as a river with a force of its own that carries us along irresistibly ('Time, like an ever-rolling stream, Bears all its sons away'). But we need not suppose that God is in the position in which we might imagine ourselves—that of standing on a bridge over a road or river, looking down at a continuous movement from past to present and on to future. When we look back upon the past we tend to visualize it as a progress in a straight line. Courses of action that we might have taken but did not, slip from the memory, and, it may be, we see everything happening in the one way that it was 'bound to happen'. But God, we may suppose, if he is omniscient, sees not only the choices we do make, and their consequences. He sees also what would be the consequences of the choices we do not make; and what would be the consequences of choices those would in their turn force us to make; and so on. God knows the actualities in the sense that he knows all the possibilities. Among those possibilities are the actualities, but we need not suppose God concerned to distinguish those possibilities that are actualities from those that are not.

Consider as an analogy the case of the chess player who can see several moves ahead, and can follow out in his mind the consequences of a number of possible courses of action. Then suppose an enormously complex electronic chess player, which can 'see' simultaneously a vast number of games all beginning from the same initial moves. Whatever happens, the electronic chess player is ready. The distinction between what its opponent actually does and what he might have done, may be said to have little or no meaning for it.

Let us leave the concept of omniscience and turn to that of omnipotence. Both these terms, it is worth remarking, are technical terms, and it is easy to forget that they are intended to express—and also, of course, to extend or to elaborate upon—features of first-hand religious experience. At least, it is reasonable to suppose that this is what they are intended basically to express. It often seems that there is a gulf between religion and theology. Theologians become immersed in the intricacies of their own subject quite as if it had nothing at all to do with the non-theoretical, non-academic religious experiences of ordinary people. This is, of course, not to say that theology ought to be nothing more than a study of such experience. This is far from the truth. Theology is 'the science of God'; a very different thing. But the science of God ought not to be divorced from first-hand religious experience.

It is hardly necessary to say that when God is said to be omnipotent this does not mean that he is 'able to do all things'. There are many things that even God cannot do. He is bound by limitations that may indeed be of his own creation but that, since they exist, are binding on all beings. He could perhaps have made a universe different from this, but, as he did not, he is bound by certain fundamental principles that apply throughout this universe. God cannot do contradictory things—cannot, for instance, simultaneously do and undo something. ('He can create and He destroy'? Yes; but only in succession. Simultaneous creation and destruction of the same thing is an idea without meaning.) God cannot do what is logically impossible. This is not to say that he cannot do what is physically 'impossible': whether there are miracles remains, so far as the present discussion is concerned, an open question. Rather than 'able to do all things' the term 'omnipotent' might perhaps be understood as meaning 'powerful over all'; that is to say, powerful as a despotic ruler is powerful, only more so. Or it might be understood as the negation of some human failings. God is omnipotent by contrast with 'weak, fallible' man. He is the Father of lights, with whom is no variableness, neither shadow of turning. He is a rock in a weary land. Men may let us down but God does not let us down. All this, of course, suggests a rather crude anthropomorphism; and on the level of religious experience, or on the biblical level, there indeed is a good deal of crude anthropomorphism. The technical term 'omnipotence' has perhaps at least the virtue of not carrying such suggestions. Certainly, when cashed in terms of such biblical language, divine omnipotence may be considered to have lost much of its terror for the believer in human free will.

CHAPTER 10

Immortality and Kindred Concepts

FURTHER support for the case against the rationality of religion seems to come from difficulties that arise in connexion with the concept of *immortality*.

The word 'immortality' has both a narrow and a wide use. The word suggests denial of death, endlessness, everlasting existence. Perhaps it has never meant only this; certainly, it does not now. To speak of a poet's writings as immortal means that they will, we hope, be remembered as long as the language in which they are written is remembered, and we do not expect this to be literally for ever. In the wider or looser use, 'immortality' is made to stand as synonym for a variety of other expressions, each of which has its own more precise definition: 'eternal life', 'survival of bodily death', 'resurrection', 'reincarnation' or 'metempsychosis', 'future life', 'life beyond the veil', 'other-worldly existence', and there are doubtless many more. In religious writings several of these expressions may occur without any attempt being made to distinguish between them, and the effect is sometimes one of confusion. It is, in particular, misleading to explain what is often called 'the Christian hope' of immortality or of everlasting life (as the Apostles' Creed says: 'I believe in . . . the life everlasting') as *really* meaning a special quality of life ('eternal life') which can be enjoyed here and now and which has no necessary reference to perpetual existence or survival of bodily death. This is not to deny the importance of the doctrine of eternal life, so understood; but what is misleading is the linking

144

of it with the phrases 'everlasting life' or 'immortality'. The effect is to imply that a particular kind of reassurance has been given that has in fact not been given.

We may generalize. 'Immortality' means, strictly, 'everlasting life'. Admittedly, the word has its wider, looser, uses; but there is always the suggestion of the narrower sense, and if this narrower sense is not intended it would make for clarity to drop the word altogether. Indeed, many religious writers would argue that a belief in strict 'immortality' is no part of Christianity, which involves instead belief in the rather different concept of 'resurrection of the body', and we need not quarrel with this; but, if this view is taken, it would surely be better if the expression 'immortality' were altogether abandoned.

A belief in survival of death or in the resurrection of the body, or in both, is an important part of religion. The connexion is not, I think, a necessary one; you may be religious without holding such beliefs or at least without holding them in any orthodox form, and you may hold such beliefs without being religious: but the connexion is nevertheless much more frequently found than not. Many people would, indeed, wish to argue that it *is* a necessary connexion. There is a mutual interaction between belief in immortality, or something of the kind, and other important religious beliefs; they act as supports for each other, and to remove one is to leave the others more inclined to topple to a passing breeze of scepticism. A chief part of the programme of anti-religious writers is often an attack on the belief in immortality. If there is no future life, there is that much less reason for believing in God. Equally, if there is no God, there is that much less reason for believing in a future life. So, at least, many people have thought.

Something more systematic must now be said about the differences in meaning between some of the key expressions that are being used here. *Immortality*, as we have already noted, when used in what we may call its strict sense, means perpetual existence. Often it is held that immortality must work in both directions—backwards as well as forwards: if there is no end to life, there is no beginning either, and the human soul has existed for ever. Unqualified belief in immortality is not particularly attractive; merely to exist for ever is hardly desirable. What may seem so is to exist in such a way as to enjoy in perpetuity experiences of a kind that we consider deeply rewarding—as, for the Christian, unending closeness to God, or, for the Muslim, the uninterrupted company of houris in Paradise.

Survival of death is the belief that when we die a bodily death the soul continues to live on, perhaps for days, perhaps for years, but probably not for ever. No belief in the soul's existence before our birth is implied here; nor, obviously, any belief in the indestructibility of the soul, as in the case of immortality. Survival of bodily death is often considered susceptible of proof by empirical methods, and some of the investigations of psychical researchers are directed to this end. By contrast, immortality in the strict sense could never be proved by any purely empirical methods, and attempts to prove it have taken the form of offering arguments of a quite non-empirical kind—metaphysical or moral arguments.

Resurrection is a specifically Christian belief, implying that death is in no sense an illusion, not an event through which we live so that the 'real person' goes on unaffected and without any temporal break at the moment of clinical death. On the contrary, *we* (as persons) do really die, our bodies decay and with their decay *we* are no more. At some future time our bodies—albeit 'glorified' bodies—are raised up and we are re-created. There is a certain amount of confusion in popular religious writings about the relation between this specifically Christian belief and belief in the soul's survival of bodily death. These two beliefs are not necessarily in all respects incompatible; not, that is, as long as the soul is not identified with the whole person or the 'real' person. But if this identification is made there is decidedly an inconsistency in the total position. The doctrine of resurrection reflects a refusal to adopt a simple dualism about human beings. It implies that the view of the human being as two things, body and soul, each capable of existing apart from the other (and of the soul as the 'real person' temporarily inhabiting a body which it may slough off without any damage to its own integrity) is mistaken, and that the better view of human personality is that it is a single whole, with, if you like, a body *aspect* and a soul *aspect* inseparable from each other. It is clear that the doctrine of survival of bodily death, with its usual implication of dualism, its implication of the soul as the 'real person' which can lose its body and continue alone without damage to its essential nature, is in conflict with this. Yet, as I have suggested, the two views may on occasion be found in alternation in the same piece of religious writing without any attempt to reconcile them.

Reincarnation or *Metempsychosis* is the doctrine—no part of Christian belief but widely held otherwise—that the soul survives bodily death but not in a discarnate form; it survives by taking up residence in another body, and after the death of that body it may move to yet another, and so on. Generally speaking, it is not held that the soul, as it thus moves from incarnation to incarnation, retains any clear memory of its previous lives. It may also be held—and indeed usually is—that nevertheless each new incarnation is determined by the manner of life of the soul in its previous incarnation, so that in the new life the soul may be expiating sins committed in the preceding life, even though they are not now remembered. It is not surprising that those peoples who have held a belief in reincarnation, or who still do, regard this cycle of reincarnation as something to be deplored rather than rejoiced over, and in their religious practices set themselves to earn escape from the Wheel of Rebirth. I shall not further consider metempsychosis, though it may be worth noting in passing that it is a belief that has been taken seriously by some eminent western philosophers.

There exist a number of arguments for immortality and for survival, but all of these presuppose something which itself needs to be argued for, and that is the truth, and even the meaningfulness, of the belief that the soul is the 'real person'. Clearly, no argument designed to show that the soul survives bodily death, whether for a limited period or for ever, can have the desired effect in the absence of agreement that the soul dissociated from the body is the real person; failing such agreement an assurance that my soul will survive will not assure me that *I* shall survive. This preliminary stage in the argument is often overlooked, because the identification of the soul alone with the 'real me' is

L

taken for granted. It cannot, however, be so taken; and the orthodox Christian insistence on the doctrine of resurrection of the body ought to be sufficient indication that the identification is not made universally.

It is perhaps hardly necessary to attempt to show that this identification is widely made, even if not by Christians with a lively sense of consistency. One literary example may suffice. Captain Ahab is lifted aboard the *Pequod* after his boat has been destroyed by Moby Dick and his ivory leg snapped off. 'Even with a broken bone, old Ahab is untouched; and I account no living bone of mine one jot more me, than this dead one that's lost. Nor white whale, nor man, nor fiend, can so much as graze old Ahab in his own proper and inaccessible being.' (The whole of this Chapter 134 of Melville's novel is interesting, as bearing upon our present theme.) Many people would be found to agree that bodily injury, to any extent, does not affect their 'proper being'; even bodily injury to the extent of death.

What does it really mean to say that the soul, which may exist disembodied, is the real or proper person? It has been argued by Professor Antony Flew (Flew and MacIntyre, pp. 269–72) that as we commonly use person words—'you', 'I', 'person', 'somebody', 'woman', etc.—they refer to entities that can be pointed at, touched, heard, seen, talked to. Yet the doctrine that the disembodied soul is the real person, if true, would involve a radically different use of person words. Disembodied souls cannot be pointed at, touched, heard, seen, talked to. It is as if while a man was alive we meant one thing by 'him', or 'John Smith', and he by 'I'; and then when he was dead we meant a different thing by 'him', or 'John Smith', and he by 'I'. The problem is one of identity. If we thus switch the meaning of person words, can we say that what, if anything, survives death is the same as the living person? Unless we can say this, there is no sense in claiming that *he*, that very person, has survived bodily death.

It should be noted that this argument is not claiming that the evidence for survival is very weak, or the evidence against it very strong. Nothing is being said about evidence. The point is a logical one, and is preliminary to any consideration of evidence. If the argument is accepted, the search for evidence will never begin; for it will have been shown that there is nothing at issue, and therefore nothing to which evidence, empirical or other, could be relevant.

This argument is, of course, powerless against someone who is willing to insist that at all times he uses and understands person words to refer only to 'the proper and inaccessible being' or soul, and never in such a way as to imply a reference, however slight and glancing, to what is seen, heard, touched. But it is doubtful whether such a person could be found; this would be an intolerably difficult programme to carry through consistently. We do not, in general, talk as if the soul, and the soul alone, were what we refer to by person words, *when we use them of living persons*. This being so, the argument stands. There is indeed a shift in the reference of person words when we move from talking of a man during his lifetime to talking of his survival of bodily death. Can we then claim that what we are talking about is the *same* person? The magnitude of the shift between meaning by 'John Smith' that man over there with such-and-such facial characteristics, mannerisms of speech and walk, such-and-such a history in space and time (studied at Oxford, lived for a time in Australia, etc.), and meaning by 'John Smith' a disembodied soul without physical characteristics or spatio-temporal history, is not to be lightly glossed over. *As we in fact use person words*, there is a gap here.

This logical argument is a strong one; and it is not without support of a more empirical kind. The criteria for personal identity are not universally agreed upon, but for our present purposes a sufficiently adequate list would be: memory, and physical continuity (continuity in space and time). At what point we are to decide when we definitely have, or when we definitely have not, a case of 'the same person' cannot be laid down in advance in general terms; but we may at least be certain that in trying to settle a difficulty of this kind we must appeal to these particular criteria. I have referred in an earlier chapter to Kafka's story *Metamorphosis*, an illuminating work on the question of personal identity. After his strange transformation, Gregor Samsa, for all the change in his appearance, retains his memory of his earlier life; to himself at least, he is still Gregor. For his parents and sister, there is the evidence of continuity in space and, they must presume, in time; one evening Gregor goes to bed, and the next morning in his room there is a strange monster —it is all very extraordinary, but the creature must be presumed to be Gregor. The point at which the real metamorphosis comes is, I think, not at the beginning of the story, but at the end; though, even so, it is not to be precisely dated. When does the giant insect cease to be Gregor Samsa? We must suppose that that moment comes when Gregor's memory of his former life finally fades (though, as it happens, there are no hints in the story that it is fading), and when he gives up hope of reconciliation with his family. But there is no single right answer to this question; and if someone were to argue that from the moment of the physical transformation Gregor Samsa ceased to exist he could not be said to be wrong.

Now in the case of death, the metamorphosis we undergo is altogether more complete than was that of Gregor Samsa. There is no physical continuity; for we know that when it has decayed in the earth or has been consumed in the crematorium fire the body is totally altered. Can there be memory? That there is a causal connexion between the brain and memory (not to mention connexion between the brain and personality traits) is fully established. With the destruction of the brain after death, how can memory survive?

It might be objected to all this that survival of bodily death is something that it is not beyond our capabilities to imagine. There are numerous well-authenticated accounts of 'out-of-the-body' experiences—in sleep, under anaesthesia, or even in waking life—in which a person feels himself leaving his body and able to look upon it as if it were the body of someone else, seeing the expression on his own face and watching people come and go around himself. We can easily imagine that survival of death might be like this—except that the experiences, unlike those of the kind just mentioned, would not be rather short-lasting; except, too, that the body the person looked back upon he would, or might, know to be dead. Whatever the empirical likelihood, or lack of it, there is at least no logical impossibility in imagining survival in some such way as this. The 'double' that is projected in out-of-the-body experiences seems to be passive or receptive; it observes action rather than originates it: and this is significant. Indeed, a disembodied existence would naturally have to be a largely passive existence; for it is by means of our bodies that we pick things up, and lay down the law, and drive a car or a hard bargain. It is not possible for a person to be disembodied and at the same time do things for which the use of the body is necessary.

The position we have reached is this. Survival of bodily death is certainly, in a sense, logically conceivable, since we can readily imagine the human consciousness as separable from the body (there is empirical evidence for this in the shape of reliable reports of out-of-the-body experiences), and we may fairly easily imagine the soul after death existing in an analogous manner. On the other hand, as we noted earlier, survival of the soul is not survival of the person, unless the disembodied soul is identified with the person. One strong reason against making this identification is that to be active and not merely passive the person would seem to need to be body as well as soul.

This last point is interesting in more ways than one. The difference between active and passive is in a way parallel to that commonly felt to exist between other people and oneself. We see other people acting. We do not experience their emotions, ideals, inner turmoils. On the other hand, we do experience, and they do not, our own emotions, ideals, inner turmoils. And we do not see ourselves acting; other people see us. All of this may take the form of a stronger conviction in a man that he himself has a soul (Do I not have direct experience of it? he may ask) than that anyone else has. As the Cartesians supposed that animals have no souls but are merely bodies, so we may suppose that other people are exhaustively accounted for in terms of their bodily behaviour; for that is what we see. The argument about the shift in meaning that person words suffer when we pass from talking about people in their lifetime to talking, if we do, about their survival of bodily death may strike us as more plausible when it is expressed in terms of 'he' than in terms of 'I'. We are more ready to agree that person words, *when used of other people*, refer to a complex in which the body plays an essential part, than to agree that this is true of such words *when used of ourselves*. It was natural for Ahab to think that damage to his body did not affect *him*—in his own proper and inaccessible being. It might have been less natural for him to think thus in the case of Starbuck or Stubb. We see ourselves 'from the inside', so we may tend to suppose that *our* history is our mental history. We see others 'from the outside', so we may tend to suppose that *their* history is their physical history. Consistency may be achieved in either direction. We may assimilate others to ourselves, or ourselves to others. But perhaps consistency is not needed. In a solipsist world each of us would be immortal, if immortal at all, to the exclusion of everybody else. It would then be a very small world, this world of the life after death; a world with one inhabitant. Though there might be many such worlds, this would be no solace to the lonely souls, each wrapped in his cocoon of silence.

What are we to conclude from the foregoing? The line of thought that we have been following is not favourable to belief in personal immortality or survival. Such a belief comes immediately up against the problem of personal identity. At least as far as other people are concerned we do not as a matter of fact consistently behave as if we thought that the body was an easily dispensable part of the person. This seems to reflect a sound appreciation of the situation. Disembodied, a soul would presumably live a life so limited on the side of activity as hardly to be identifiable with normal life. It would be like a life of complete bodily paralysis—which would not be easily distinguishable from death.

So far nothing has been said about the arguments that are offered in support of a belief in immortality. If the considerations put forward so far in this chapter are accepted, it is necessary to conclude that the concept of personal immortality is a doubtfully meaningful one; and arguments for a belief, however apparently strong in themselves, can hardly do much to establish it if there is reason to suppose the belief itself fundamentally confused. As it happens, the arguments for immortality are not in any case particularly strong ones.

However, if we are to do justice to the arguments for immortality we must not rule out, *a priori*, the possibility that they might succeed. They must be given a fair chance, and we must be prepared, if necessary, to reconsider the case against survival that has been outlined in the earlier part of this chapter. There certainly can be no doubt that many people do believe in survival of death. Certainly, many people *wish* for it. In such a favourable climate an argument for survival does not need to be strong to be accepted. At the same time, to approach the arguments with a mind already fixed in a sceptical frame is to deny them the chance to show even the degrees of strength they do have.

We have earlier noted the distinction between empirical arguments for survival and metaphysical or moral arguments. Basically, there is only one empirical argument, but it has many parts. It consists in an appeal to phenomena of the kind investigated by psychical researchers. Phenomena of clairvoyance, telepathy, precognition, and psycho-kinesis, though not in themselves directly relevant to the proof of survival, are perhaps indirectly relevant as suggesting what form such a life could take. If we accept these phenomena as well-established—and this need not be disputed, though they are not all in fact equally well-established—the picture of the future life sketched earlier seems unnecessarily austere. It perhaps need not, on this supposition, after all, be a purely solitary and passive life: perhaps communication between discarnate souls could take place, and perhaps they could act upon each other—though this, of course, depends upon precisely what part is played by the body.

The phenomena that may be considered directly relevant to the question of survival of death are rather different. Out-of-the-body experiences, it might be suggested, are relevant. So, indeed, they may be; but it must be remembered that these are experiences enjoyed by people who are alive and who 'return to their physical bodies' at the end of the experience. More significantly, there is the phrase used frequently in accounts of these experiences, 'the silver cord', as the name of the 'link' between the person and his double. If this 'silver cord' is itself merely the reflection of a particular theory about the experience too much weight should not be put upon it. But if it is to be taken as part of the first-hand account of the experience itself it is clearly very significant, suggesting as it does that the personality, though disembodied, is felt to be still essentially linked to the body. This would considerably weaken the force of an appeal to out-of-the-body experiences as part of the case for survival. It does seem from recorded cases in which this experience of a 'link' is reported, that it is part of the first-hand experience itself.

The phenomena discussed by psychical researchers under the name of 'apparitions' and 'materializations' may seem to offer *prima facie* evidence for survival of death. Now, what is immediately striking about these—and this is largely true also of out-of-the-body experiences—is the tacit acknowledgement they seem to make of the importance of the body. Apparitions are *seen*, materializations are *seen and touched*. Perhaps in this there is a kind of unconscious tribute to the Christian doctrine of resurrection. It is as if we want to have it both ways. I except the members of the Society for Psychical Research and others who aim expressly to approach this question without preconceived ideas; but as far as the general public is concerned, survival is, I think, usually understood in the sense of survival of the non-bodily, non-material part of the human person—the soul or spirit; and yet in looking for evidence ordinary people are probably impressed most by what on the surface would seem to be evidence for the survival of the body, if they did not know that this is just what has not survived, rather than for the survival of the soul. The incongruity of the wearing of clothes by apparitions of dead persons has sometimes been remarked on (Do trousers and shirts have souls, too? it has been asked); but in reality there should be something just as incongruous about the apparition or materialization of a naked human body, on the assumption that it is the non-material soul that survives. I do not deny the well-attested character of accounts of apparitions; though materializations are by no means so well-evidenced. The question is really whether, supposing them for our present purposes both well-evidenced, they can possibly prove what they are often said to prove. There is also the point, which ought not to be overlooked, that the clothes worn by apparitions can be accounted for in terms of memory-images in the mind of the observer: but, if so, may not the apparitions and materializations themselves be accounted for in the same way? I do not assert that they can; but this is at least a possibility.

One would expect, in the light of what has just been said, that stronger evidence for survival might be found in the realm of phenomena of a less blatantly bodily character. This is in fact so. Mediumistic communication is the obvious type of case to be considered here. The complex case of cross-correspondences offers even more impressive *prima facie* evidence. This is the type of case in which a number of automatists are involved who, without contact with each other, produce complementary scripts containing out-of-the-way information that it is certain was possessed by only a very few people including the dead man who is ostensibly communicating it. An explanation of most mediumistic phenomena in terms of clairvoyance, or telepathic communication from the living, is generally possible, which obviates the necessity of supposing survival of death. Cross-correspondences are not so easily accounted for, however, and must, I think, be allowed to stand as *prima facie* evidence for survival.

Other phenomena of a character more 'mental' than 'material' —like the evidence for 'extra-sensory perception' claimed by Professor J. B. Rhine and others—have, as I remarked earlier in the chapter, some indirect value in indicating what 'life after death', supposing there to be such a thing, might be like, or, we might now add, in weakening the tendency to a 'materialistic' outlook and encouraging an atmosphere in which belief in survival is not rejected out of hand; but they do not have any direct evidential force towards proving survival.

The foregoing discussion of the many-headed empirical argument for survival has been, of necessity, brief; and it would be wrong to draw dogmatic conclusions from it. Much further argument would be required to justify a conclusion that the case for survival is definitely proved, or definitely disproved, on the basis of the putative evidence that we have been examining.

The metaphysical and moral arguments for immortality need not occupy us for as long as did the empirical argument. There are a number of metaphysical arguments for immortality—and

they are arguments for immortality and not merely for survival—
but they generally have in common the view of the soul as a
substance, separable from the body, another substance. To talk of
a person's mental and physical welfare would, on this view, be to
talk not about different parts of his welfare but about the welfare
of literally different parts of him. The soul, it is held, is a special
kind of substance, not extended and divisible, as is the body, but
unextended, 'a thinking thing', indivisible. The soul, it would
sometimes be said, is a *simple* substance. It is in this that the proof
of its immortality may be made to lie; as, for instance, by
Descartes. Operating, as he does, with a sharp distinction between
body and soul, in which their difference may be said, at least in
part, to lie in the complexity of the one (which thus is able to
break up into its constituent parts, i.e. to decay, to die) as
contrasted with the simplicity of the other (which, having no
parts, cannot break up, i.e. which cannot decay, die), Descartes
has no difficulty in establishing the immortality of the soul;
though his procedure is likely to strike the reader as less a
demonstration of the immortality of the soul than a loud and
confident assertion of it.

The concept of substance is nowadays under a philosophical
cloud. It is not easy to understand precisely what is meant by
calling the soul a simple substance. Certainly, if the soul is simple
rather than complex, whatever exactly this may mean, and if
death does consist in the breaking up of a thing into its constituent
parts, the soul, having no parts, must be immortal. But the
difficulty is one of understanding this way of talking. If the soul
is identified with the mind, as it was by Descartes, it is difficult
to see what is meant by saying that it is simple. On any commonsense level the mind is highly complex: we need think only of the
wide variety of mental acts—of memory, imagination, will,
intellect. It may be said that this objection is naïve; for what is
meant by the simplicity of the soul is not that it is simple in
function but that it is a simple substance, whereas the body is a
complex substance. The reply must be that it is still far from clear
that there is any such difference. Of course, one may *say* that the
soul is a simple substance; but this kind of terminology is un-
profitable. 'Simplicity' seems little more than a defining character-

istic of the soul, with no real cash-value of its own. Part, indeed, of what meaning it has is, I think, precisely indestructibility, deathlessness; so that to appeal to the soul's simplicity *in proof of* its immortality is to beg the question. It is perhaps proper to note that those who use this terminology do not always want to speak of the soul as a *separate* substance; they may speak of the soul (or 'consciousness', 'life', etc.) as a qualification of the single substance that we are—we are 'animated bodies'. This way of putting things does not help towards the proof of immortality. Indeed, it is a positive hindrance. Either, if we are to use this terminology, the soul is a substance in its own right, or it is a qualification of the substance that is the whole human being. If it is the latter, it can hardly exist alone in any case; if the former, the question of its immortality is still unproved, unless we beg the question by defining it as 'simple', meaning 'indivisible' or 'indestructible'. In short, the concept of substance is as much a hindrance as a help in proving the immortality of the soul.

Not all metaphysical arguments for the immortality of the soul need be of just this kind; but I shall not spend time on other such arguments but pass at once to moral arguments. We have noted in an earlier chapter Kant's moral argument for immortality. God, freedom, and immortality are 'postulates of the practical reason'. Most moral arguments for immortality follow Kantian lines. It is argued that without a future life morality would not 'make sense'. Sometimes the existence of God is an additional premise in the argument. It is argued that because there is a God, who is the moral governor of the universe, and because morality is somehow incomplete in this life (virtue going unrewarded, vice unpunished, etc.), there must be a future life. A moral argument of this form can have little cogency for someone who is not already a believer in God. We have noted already how belief in God and belief in immortality tend to go together, and how the holding of one prepares the ground for the other; but for the man who begins by believing in neither it is unlikely that either will seem initially more attractive than the other. In the form that Kant gives it—where both God and immortality are seen to follow together from morality—the argument at least assumes less.

The moral argument for immortality stands or falls according to whether one accepts its premise about the incompleteness of 'this-worldly' morality. To the believer in God this incompleteness will tend to seem self-evident. Kant himself, we must remember, was a believer in God, and although he did not formally make the existence of God a premise of his moral argument for immortality, it is reasonable to suppose that if he had not in fact believed in God he would never have been so strongly impressed by the 'incompleteness' of earthly morality. If we consider the matter in isolation from belief in God, it is far from self-evident that there is anything incomplete about this-worldly morality. Certainly, in this life virtue is not always rewarded and vice is not always punished; but perhaps that is just the way things are. We are often enough told that virtue is its own reward—which is, perhaps, an acknowledgement that we need not expect any reward whatever. For that matter, ought we to expect any? Certainly, as Kant himself insisted, if we act *for the sake of reward*, whether in this life or in another, it is questionable whether we can be said to be acting virtuously at all. Kant, we remember, held that happiness is part of man's supreme good —happiness on condition of virtue—and this view is appealing. But this of itself would not entitle us to consider a future life proved. It would be more reasonable to conclude that more often than not men never achieve their supreme good.

So much for the metaphysical and moral arguments. There are also some arguments of a more specifically Christian character —from the Resurrection of Christ, or from the experience of a special relationship to God—but these I shall not discuss. They fall under the general comment I have made about the way in which prior belief in God makes belief in immortality congenial, and I do not think they bring to the matter any powerfully new *arguments*. What perhaps they do is rather to underline the fact that belief in immortality is seldom if ever something that people argue themselves or others into; the belief—or faith—comes first, and arguments, if any, follow after.

Although I shall not here consider the argument from the Resurrection of Christ, the concept of resurrection itself calls for a word or two of comment. One of the meanings borne by 'immortality' in the wide sense is what Christians call 'resurrection of the body'. Sometimes the expression 'general resurrection' is used to distinguish this from the Resurrection of Christ. This belief, even if not in precisely the Christian form, has a long pre-Christian history, and is one variety of the general belief in immortality that, at least on the surface, seems to avoid the chief difficulty that faces belief in the indefinite survival of the soul in isolation from the body; for if there were to be indeed a re-creation of the person—a re-uniting of soul and body, to put it in Dualist language—there would be less difficulty in supposing that it was *I* who survived my bodily death. Belief in reincarnation would have the same advantage, if it were not for the problem set by our apparent failure to carry over memories from one life to the next.

The doctrine of resurrection avoids one difficulty only at the cost of creating others. In particular, there is an obvious problem of meaning here. What exactly can be meant by the resurrection of the body? Hardly the literal resurrection of the physical body. The Christian view is that what is resurrected is a *spiritual* body, and this clearly calls for explanation.

Let us bring this discussion of immortality to an end. What has finally emerged from it?

Immortality is not conclusively established by any of the arguments I have considered, and I think those I have examined are the main ones. Further, the logical considerations of the earlier part of the chapter seem to constitute *prima facie* grounds for holding that the whole notion of survival of death is incoherent. So far, then, we may say that belief in immortality is irrational; and in so far as this belief is a part of religion to that extent religion is irrational.

Like so much in religion, belief in immortality is determined by hopes and aspirations, by wishes of various kinds. There is a sense of 'rational' in which it is rational to accept what makes for peace of mind; the rational man comes to terms with himself. If by 'rational' we mean not 'adequately supported by arguments, consistent, etc.' but 'commending itself as a resolution of natural human hopes, etc.', belief in immortality may well be called 'rational'. This comes perilously close to saying that it is rational to believe what one wants to believe, and the dangers of this doctrine are sufficiently obvious to make this a sense of 'rational' not to be recommended. The value of a belief in immortality is in any case not as great as is sometimes supposed. An appeal to a future life can too easily be made the excuse for failure to take this life seriously enough.

CHAPTER 11

Some Psychological Themes

ONE of the strongest influences towards the establishing of the contemporary view of religion has been that of psychology. This is only one effect of the growing importance of scientific attitudes; for it is with its graduation from being a middle-aged partner of philosophy to a junior place among the sciences that psychology has come to have an effect upon men's views about religion. In this chapter I propose to discuss some aspects of this effect.

It is in the work of Freud that the case against reason in religion receives the form in which it has probably made the widest and deepest impression on the contemporary educated mind. Religion is irrational for Freud in the sense that it is a kind of neurosis. As he said more than once, it is a universal neurosis, and valuable to the extent that it may prevent personal neuroses. But he is not really interested in encouraging its survival, and looks to the day when, as he puts it, the consequences of repression—religious dogmas—will be replaced by the results of rational mental effort.

Religion, then, is a kind of neurosis, and a neurotic person is an irrational person. Freud's 1907 paper on 'Obsessive Actions and Religious Practices' makes the point clearly. There he says that obsessive acts express *unconscious* motives and ideas, and he suggests that the motives impelling the ordinary religious believer to religious practices are unknown to him or are 're-placed in consciousness by others which are advanced in their stead'. It is, Freud thinks, the origin of religion in the unconscious that makes it irrational. To use his later terminology, religion is the product of the Pleasure-Pain Principle and not of the Reality Principle.

But it is in *The Future of an Illusion* (1927) that his ideas have had their most influential expression. His general view here is that religion originates in the infantile helplessness of man; not a new idea, and for that matter not necessarily an irreligious one, and Freud claims no originality for it, saying merely that he is able to offer strong reinforcement for it from the findings of psycho-analysis. He inquires to what circumstances religious doctrines owe their efficacy, 'independent, as it is, of the acknowledgement of the reason'. Religion is an *illusion*; but it is an illusion in a rather special sense. 'An illusion is not the same as an error, it is indeed not necessarily an error.' An illusion is a belief deriving from men's wishes. 'For instance, a poor girl may have an illusion that a prince will come and fetch her home. It is possible; some such cases have occurred.' 'Thus we call a belief an illusion when wish-fulfilment is a prominent factor in its motivation, while disregarding its relations to reality, just as the illusion itself does.' The influence of our wishes on our religious beliefs is obvious, Freud thinks. We would like to think that there is a benevolent deity, and a future life, and all the rest of it.

It should be noted that Freud does not claim to have shown that religious beliefs are false. They may be true—as may be the poor girl's belief that a prince will come for her. But, he would claim, where a belief is obviously strongly influenced by the wishes of the believer we do right to feel suspicion. To believe something because it would be very nice if it were true is not to believe it on rational grounds. Freud supposes that a belief which is, in his odd and rather tendentious sense, an illusion, is likely to be untrue, even though it may not be possible to show that it is certainly untrue.

Now it is clear that where there is good independent evidence for a given belief, the fact that people may also hold that belief because they want to is neither here nor there. If there were good independent evidence for the existence of God or for a future life, then the fact that many people want to believe in God or in a future life would doubtless seem of no great importance. It assumes importance only if it is supposed that there is no good independent evidence for these things. Freud does, of course, suppose this. He is on strong ground in so doing. In the absence of a prior inclination to believe, there is not a great deal which would strike anyone today as clear and indubitable evidence for the existence of God: this is a point that I made frequently in the course of the earlier discussion of the standard theistic proofs. If, on the other hand, a man is predisposed to interpret his experience theistically—perhaps because of childhood teaching or for some other reason—he is a great deal more likely to find what he would claim to be evidence for the truth of theism. This is no more than common sense.

The question, 'Is there good objective evidence for the existence of God or for a future life (or for any other item of religious belief)?' is not a simple one. The theist would claim that there is such evidence. Freud would claim that there is not. It is not possible to adjudicate between them immediately. What strikes one man as evidence does not so strike another man. From Freud's point of view there is no good independent evidence for the truth of religion; and he is consequently justified in concluding that, as he sees it, the wishful character of religious belief constitutes ground for a rational man's having nothing to do with it.

There are two important features of Freud's thought that need to be discussed fairly fully.

Ernest Jones, in his biography of Freud, has laid stress on his interest in *history*, and in how man came to be civilized man. He was greatly interested in primitive peoples; and was also much taken up with Greek and Roman civilization, and tended to refer to it for illumination on other things. His choice of the expression 'Oedipus complex' is the obvious instance of this. His general interest in the origins of things was certainly a determining factor in the adoption of the particular therapeutic methods that he did adopt.

The effect of this on his views about religion is noticeable. He seems concerned with the past of religion rather than with its present; or when he is concerned with its present it is often with forms of religion that would be called—by Freud as much as by anyone else—'primitive', a word which carries with it the implication of survival from the past. There are exceptions to this lack of interest in the present forms of 'developed' religion, but, by and

M

large, this restriction of his interest is marked. It is the *beginnings* of Judaism and Christianity that attract him, how they came to be what they are; and it is the coming to be rather than the being in which he is really interested. His interest in the origins of religion in the individual is of a similar sort. He is not greatly inclined to consider the different types of religious person—the muscular Christian, say, as opposed to the weak seeker after an undefined comfort, or the Quaker as opposed to the Anglo-Catholic. For Freud, the religion of all these is equally to be explained in terms of the Oedipus complex. Modern analysts, it is fair to say, are by no means committed to agreeing with him on this.

Basically, Freud, like all men who have discovered an important explanatory concept, is attempting to explain the complicated in terms of the simple, the many in terms of the one. There is perhaps a natural tendency to think that things become simpler if you go back in time, that the origins of things are less complicated than their subsequent, developed, forms. Freud had no deep personal interest in religion. (At least, he claimed that he had none; but his attitude towards religion was highly ambivalent.) There is clearly a connexion between this lack of personal interest in religion—he told Ernest Jones that he had never believed in a supernatural world, and, says Jones, 'went through his life from beginning to end as a natural atheist'—and his view that it must be possible to give some quite simple explanation of it. His curiosity about the origins of things completes the picture. He himself might have denied this. 'There are no grounds for fearing that psycho-analysis, which first discovered that psychical acts and structures are invariably overdetermined, will be tempted to trace the origin of anything so complicated as religion to a single source' (Freud (2), p. 100). Yet, despite this disclaimer, I think it is possible to detect in him a belief in one simple basic explanation of religion—and not only of religion. 'At the conclusion, then, of this exceedingly condensed inquiry, I should like to insist that its outcome shows that the beginnings of religion, morals, society and art converge in the Oedipus complex. . . . It seems to me a most surprising discovery that the problems of social psychology . . . should prove soluble on the basis of one single concrete point—man's relation to his father, (*ibid.*, p. 156).

The Christian believer may be tempted to dismiss this out of hand, as involving the committing of the genetic fallacy—the fallacy that the final value of a thing is entirely determined by the value of its origins; as if, to take a crude example, a man might say that Coleridge's 'Kubla Khan' is not worth treating seriously as a poem because it originated in an opium dream, and opium taking is something to be deprecated. But this would be too facile. Simply to invoke the genetic fallacy is to take up too clumsy a weapon; for there certainly are cases where discovery of its origins does seem to be relevant to a possible reassessment of the value of a thing—like discovering an abstract painting to have been done by a chimpanzee, or a poem to have been concocted for a joke by the stringing together of phrases from a newspaper. Each case needs to be considered on its merits. Furthermore, to suppose that what we think of as 'developed' religions must, because they are developed, be impossible of adequate explanation in terms drawn wholly from primitive religions, may be to beg the question; for part of what is at issue is whether or not what are *called* 'developed' religions are really anything more than primitive religions in disguise. Certainly, as Freud views them, they are nothing more than this.

It is necessary to distinguish between Freud's theory of the historical origins of religion among mankind in the remote past (which he expounds in *Totem and Taboo*) and his theory of its psychological origins in the individual here and now (best seen, as I have already said, in *The Future of an Illusion*). These theories differ in some respects, as he himself recognizes. In the former the stress is on the expiation of guilt, whereas in the latter it is more on 'infantile helplessness' and 'wish-fulfilment'. His theory of the historical origins of religion has as much bearing on the question of the rationality of religion as has the better-known Freudian theory of its psychological origins. What is at issue at present is the question how far any account of religion in terms of its origins may be taken as offering an adequate explanation of religion. Everything, of course, depends on the form the account takes. Let us consider Freud's account of the *psychological* origins of religion—as constituting the best-known, and the most characteristic, thing in Freud's numerous discussions of religion.

Now we have here, it seems, an explanation of religion that carries a considerable degree of plausibility, certainly as applied to some sorts of religious people. The terms in which Freudian accounts of religion have been given—involving not only the notions of wish-fulfilment and infantility but also notions like those of 'father substitute' or 'sublimated sex'—are certainly illuminating when used of certain religious people, both clerical and lay.

It is sometimes made a matter of complaint against Freud that his theory is not empirically verifiable; or, contrariwise, that it is empirically verifiable, and that investigations seem to show that it is false. Certainly, if this is to be taken as a serious scientific theory, questions about its empirical verifiability would need to be raised, and the answers might well be unfavourable to Freud. But I am doubtful whether—whatever its author himself intended —this theory ought to be regarded as a scientific theory. The model that lies behind it is that of history, not science; and history regarded as an art—and not as itself a kind of science—in which speculation about a given situation may illuminatingly play over its supposed origins, certainly not without reference to the facts, as far as they are known, but at the same time without being too closely wedded to those facts. It has been suggested that Freud should be thought of as a literary artist rather than as a scientist, and he was in fact a remarkably good writer. We do not reject the insights into human nature and human institutions of a great novelist or dramatist if they do not pass scientific tests. We accept them as illuminating, without considering for one moment the application of such tests; and our instinct in this is surely right.

The relationship between Freud's theories about religion and his clinical findings is tenuous, to say the least. Certainly his views on religion are not entailed by psycho-analysis. He might have put forward much the same views if he had never been the founder of psycho-analysis; and no present-day analyst is committed to holding them because the founder held them. Neither Freud nor Jung, to the discussion of whose views I turn later in the chapter, in putting forward his ideas about religion, is advancing theories capable of being conclusively demonstrated by empirical evidence, whatever he himself may think. The best way of regarding them both is as imaginative writers, who have thrown new light on a fundamentally important aspect of life much as a great novelist might do.

Freud's importance, as an influence tending towards the spread of the view of religion as non-rational, is of the very greatest. He provides this view with no cast-iron logical support; but the kind of support he does provide, like that provided to any view by an imaginative writer of genius, is at least as effective in practice.

We have noted Freud's interest in history, and, in general, in the origins of things. The other striking feature of his thought that calls for comment is his literal-mindedness. This comes out clearly in his theory in *Totem and Taboo* of the historical origins of religion.

Here Freud elaborates on ideas put forward by Darwin, J. J. Atkinson, and W. Robertson Smith. Men originally lived in small groups—'primal hordes'—under the rule of a father. All the women were at the father's disposal and his sons were excluded from them. The sons hated the father as an obstacle to their desire for power and their sexual desires, but at the same time they looked up to him and admired him. Eventually they rose in revolt, killed the father and ate him, and took the women (their mothers) for themselves. But then remorse overtook them, and a sense of guilt made its appearance. Out of this sense of guilt came the two primitive taboos—against murder and against incest.

From this remorse and sense of guilt arises also religion, in the form of totemism—'a first attempt at a religion'. The totem is a substitute for the father. 'The totemic system was, as it were, a covenant with their father, in which he promised them everything that a childish imagination may expect from a father—protection, care, and indulgence—while on their side they undertook to respect his life, that is to say, not to repeat the deed which brought destruction on their real father . . . . Totemic religion arose from the filial sense of guilt, in an attempt to allay that feeling and to appease the father by deferred obedience to him. All later religions are seen to be attempts at solving the same problem.

They vary according to the stage of civilization at which they arise and according to the methods which they adopt; but all have the same end in view and are reactions to the same great event with which civilization began and which, since it occurred, has not allowed mankind a moment's rest' (Freud (2), p. 144).

Freud makes some particular applications of these ideas to Christianity. In 'the Christian myth' the original sin can only have been murder; for Christ sacrificed his life and 'self-sacrifice points back to blood-guilt'. But through this self-sacrifice Christ himself became God. (How exactly this happened is not made clear.) 'A son-religion displaced the father-religion.' The ancient totem-feast was revived as the Communion, 'in which the company of brothers consumed the flesh and blood of the son—no longer the father—obtained sanctity thereby and identified themselves with him'. 'The Christian communion, however, is essentially a fresh elimination of the father, a repetition of the guilty deed.'

Whether Darwin's story about early societies is true no one knows or could know. The significant thing is that Freud himself takes it as historical truth—though not as the story of an event that happened once and once only; for some such events as these, he considers, must have been repeated many times. His insistence on the literal truth of this account of the origins of religion is to be noted. The insistence is unfortunate. The story may be true, but nothing in fact hangs upon its truth. 'About these happenings there can be little doubt: fathers, gods, and kings have been slain innumerable times in the tragic history of mankind,' says Ernest Jones, commenting on Freud. Yes; certainly. But it is not the mere slaying of fathers and kings that is in question; nor the mere slaying of gods. The slaying of 'gods', indeed, suggests the sort of mythological or symbolical 'truth' which the Darwinian story has; and it is this that matters, not the literal truth of the story. Freud would certainly not be content with mythological or symbolical truth. (As the term 'symbolical' will be used in a somewhat special sense in the following chapter I should perhaps say that in the present chapter I do not intend it in any technical sense.)

Freud's insistence on the literalness of the story drives him into metaphysics—into the postulation of a collective mind, 'in which mental processes occur just as they do in the mind of an individual' (p. 157), and in which the sense of guilt remains for thousands of years. This has a decidedly Jungian sound; and, indeed, when he was writing *Totem and Taboo* Freud was greatly interested in Jung's views on religion. At first he was impressed by Jung's work, but later came to think his own would bring to a head the differences between them. It is significant that one of the reasons that Freud gives in his *History of the Psycho-Analytic Movement* for the break between himself and Jung was the latter's tendency to interpret the Oedipus complex as having a 'merely' symbolical or anagogic meaning. He suggests that the 'theological prehistory' of 'so many of the Swiss' throws light on Jung's attitude to psycho-analysis. Religion and morality are regarded by Jung with too much respect, and an account of their origins in sexual terms seems not quite the thing; hence Jung's tendency to interpret these origins in a non-literal way. Freud, admittedly, at times allows his imagination free play, and is prepared to see what we can call symbolical meanings in what might be thought everyday events; but, for all that, there is a literal-mindedness about him which in his own eyes marks a clear difference between him and Jung. (In the 1907 paper on 'Obsessive Actions and Religious Practices' he had been more willing to speak of symbolical meaning.)

It seems that for Freud it is important to recognize that the historical origins of religion were in real events of the kind described—events that really happened. When he discusses its psychological origins, similarly, he insists on the reality of the infant's ambivalent attitude of love and hatred of his father and the reality of his desire for sexual intercourse with his mother. It would be absurd to say that Freud does not recognize that there are *fantasies* in infancy; for this is precisely one of the things that he was the first clearly to recognize—like his early patients' 'memories' of rape by their relatives—but the Oedipus complex as he understands it basically originates in *real* events of infancy— real attitudes and real feelings, that is. Though it ought perhaps to be added that it is not altogether clear what 'real events' of infancy Freud has in mind. What are real attitudes and real feelings? What kind of unreality is being excluded?

He ends *Totem and Taboo* by reverting explicitly to the comparison between primitives and neurotics which had been the idea giving direction to the book throughout; its subtitle is: 'Some Points of Agreement between the Mental Lives of Savages and Neurotics'. 'It is not accurate to say that obsessional neurotics, weighed down under the burden of an excessive morality, are defending themselves only against *psychical* reality and are punishing themselves for impulses which were merely *felt*. *Historical* reality has a share in the matter as well. In their childhood they had these evil impulses pure and simple, and turned them into acts so far as the impotence of childhood allowed. Each of these excessively virtuous individuals passed through an evil period in his infancy—a phase of perversion which was the forerunner and precondition of the later period of excessive morality. The analogy between primitive men and neurotics will therefore be far more fully established if we suppose that in the former instance, too, psychical reality—as to the form taken by which we are in no doubt—coincided at the beginning with factual reality: that primitive men actually *did* what all the evidence shows that they intended to do . . . . Primitive men . . . are *uninhibited*: thought passes directly into action . . . . And that is why, without laying claim to any finality of judgement, I think that in the case before us it may safely be assumed that "in the beginning was the Deed" ' (p. 160–1).

'Primitive men actually *did* what all the evidence shows that they intended to do.' The origins of religion are in historical events. Yet religion is still, for Freud, fundamentally a neurosis and irrational.

Freud's notion of the pathological character of much guilt has begun to have an effect on Christian writers (see, e.g. Vidler, pp. 52–4); though, ironically, this coincides with a tendency among some psychologists themselves to react from Freud in the direction of admitting the naturalness and importance of guilt feelings (see Mowrer).

From Freud we pass to C. G. Jung (1875–1961). What I chiefly wish to do here is to underline the contrast already noted between Freud's stress on literal meaning and Jung's on symbolical meaning. This contrast is of some importance for our central theme—the place of reason in religion. The contrast is usefully illustrated by the following Jungian comment (by Fr. Victor White) on Freud: 'It need hardly be said that there is no Scriptural or historic warrant for the myth of the murder of Moses whereby he accounts for the guilt-sense of the Jewish race; but this postulate of the murder of the Lawgiver may not unreasonably be interpreted as a symbolic expression of disobedience to the Mosaic Law. Freud's myth of the primeval parricide, in which the brothers slew the Father, usurped his power and took his wives, may be read as a weird secularization of the Genesis story. For here the collective Man (Adam) indeed slays his Father, in the sense that he kills the divine life of the God within him, usurps his power ("Ye shall be as God") and takes possession of his own soul—the *anima* which God has made to be his companion' (Mairet, p. 171, footnote).

Jung's interest in symbolical meaning springs from his hypothesis of the collective unconscious and of primitive archetypes as its 'contents'. He writes of the connexion of 'spontaneous modern symbolism' with 'ancient theories and beliefs', and says: 'Such a continuity can only exist if we assume a certain unconscious condition as an inherited *a priori* factor. By this I naturally do not mean the inheritance of ideas, which would be difficult if not impossible to prove. I suppose, rather, the inherited quality to be something like the formal possibility of producing the same or similar ideas over and over again. I have called this possibility the "archetype". Accordingly, the archetype would be a structural quality or condition peculiar to a psyche that is somehow connected with the brain' (Jung (2), p. 103–4).

In the statement of his views that he contributed as a Foreword to Fr. White's *God and the Unconscious* Jung is characteristically unclear about the status of archetypes. The following two passages, which are separated from each other by only a couple of inches of print, express points of view that are by no means the same. 'Nevertheless, it is possible that there are—as is the case with other metaphysical statements, particularly the dogmas—archetypal factors in the background here [he has been discussing the view of evil as *privatio boni*] which have existed for an infinitely long time as psychically effective, pre-forming factors; *and these would be accessible to empirical research* [my italics].' 'Like every empirical science, psychology also requires auxiliary concepts, hypotheses and models. But the theologian, as well as the philosopher, is apt to make the mistake of taking them for metaphysical *a priori* assertions. The atom of which the physicist speaks is not a metaphysical hypothesis, it is a *model*. Similarly, my concept of the archetype or of psychic energy is [my italics now:] *only an auxiliary idea, which can be exchanged at any time for a better formula*' (White, pp. xx–xxi). Now it is true that there is a difference between 'metaphysical *a priori* assertions' and scientific hypotheses, 'models', or 'auxiliary ideas': it is equally true, however, that the logical status of scientific hypotheses, models, or auxiliary ideas is not the same as that of empirical statements —and although Jung does recognize this, in the second of the two passages, it is odd that the man who wrote that passage should have been capable also of writing the other. The contents of people's minds can be said to be open to empirical investigation; but that these contents express *archetypes* is not establishable empirically—here we are in the realm of hypotheses or 'auxiliary ideas'. The hypotheses, models, or auxiliary concepts of an empirical science are not themselves objects of empirical investigation by that science: they are the ideas by the use of which order is imposed on the things that *are* the objects of empirical investigation by that science. Jung is noticeably fond of calling himself an 'empiricist'. In his eagerness to insist on this he is sometimes in danger of falling into the error of thinking that all the propositions that go to make up an empirical study must be empirical propositions. In the second of the two passages just quoted he has quickly recovered the footing missed in the first; but the tendency to stumble again in the same way is never far distant. If the archetypes *were* 'accessible to empirical research', as he says they are, Jung's psychology would run the risk of becoming simply a classificatory or descriptive study. If they are to have any explanatory force it will not do for them to be themselves the objects of empirical investigation; they must be (as he himself claims them to be in the second passage—which certainly expresses his real, unconfused, view) hypotheses, or 'auxiliary

ideas', in terms of which we may attempt to explain what we
empirically observe.

Religion is non-rational for Jung in the sense that it is a
product of the unconscious, as it was for Freud, though for Jung
it is a product of the *collective* unconscious. Religious symbols
symbolize archetypes, and archetypes belong to the pre-rational
psyche. Jung's interest in symbolical meaning is perhaps mainly
to be distinguished from the similar interest displayed by Christian writers of all ages by the fact that he spreads his net more
widely than they. Where they on the whole seek to link Christian
symbols with other symbols that have some historical or conscious
connexion with them, Jung's device of the collective unconscious
enables him to make plausible links (plausible, that is, in the
context of Jungian theory) between symbols that have no
historical or conscious connexion with each other.

The modern revival of interest among certain theologians in
biblical imagery and symbolism and in typology leads to writers,
who are not, one would have thought, particularly under his
influence, saying things that might have been said by Jung. In
case the reader may wish for an example let him reflect on this
passage from Professor E. L. Mascall's *Christ, the Christian and the
Church*: 'But, asks Hoskyns, why did Christ appear in a form that
could be mistaken for that of the gardener? The answer is, because
he *was* the Gardener: the Adam placed in the garden by the
Father in order that it should bring forth its fruits, and also the
supreme and original Gardener, the Lord Jehovah who had
planted the Garden eastward in Eden' (p. 138). This sort of
thing is a godsend to preachers. Perhaps it is literally a godsend,
as Professor Mascall seems to think: 'The imagery of the cloud
and trumpets is a symbolical form of words providentially
provided by God through the medium of Jewish apocalyptic'
(Mascall (1), p. 105).

Whereas Freud was greatly concerned about the *truth* of
religion Jung was hardly so concerned at all. Jung is generally
considered more sympathetic to religion than Freud, and so
indeed he is—that is, as far as intention goes. But Jung may be a
more dangerous ally than Freud an enemy, and those Christian
writers who have attempted the difficult task of Christianizing

Freud may be wiser than those who have gratefully taken over
large pieces of Jung. The view of religion as 'neither true nor
false', or as 'true only in a special sense' (symbolically true,
psychologically true) has shortcomings. Freud, with his apparently
naïve literal-minded idea that religion must be either true or false,
and in no special senses of 'true' or 'false', is clinging to something
that religious believers, as much as non-believers like himself,
ought not to neglect. Jung does not ask whether religious dogmas
are true; he asks what other symbols can be linked with them,
and he asks what religion *does*. What religion does, he finds, is to
assist towards integration. To those who cannot accept the
Christian metaphysic he offers a metaphysic whose acceptance
may bring integration through the realization of the archetypes
in other, not orthodox Christian, forms. Religion, after all, is so
many things. . . . The value of religion for Jung is pragmatic—
though that he holds this is denied by some of his followers. 'No
matter what the world thinks about religious experience, the one
who has it possesses a great treasure, a thing that has become for
him a source of life, meaning, and beauty, and that has given a
new splendour to the world and to mankind. He has *pistis* and
peace. Where is the criterion by which you could say that such a
life is not legitimate, that such an experience is not valid, and
that such *pistis* is mere illusion? Is there, as a matter of fact, any
better truth about the ultimate things than the one that helps you
to live? . . . The thing that cures a neurosis must be as convincing
as the neurosis, and since the latter is only too real, the helpful
experience must be equally real. It must be a very real illusion,
if you want to put it pessimistically. But what is the difference
between a real illusion and a healing religious experience? It is
merely a difference of words. . . . No one can know what the
ultimate things are. We must therefore take them as we experience
them. And if such experience helps to make life healthier, more
beautiful, more complete and more satisfactory to yourself and
to those you love, you may safely say: "This was the grace of
God" ' (Jung (2), p. 105).

I do not wish to reject out of hand a view of religion that sees
its value as lying in 'making life healthier', and so on. Such a
view is, I think, inadequate. A man may certainly say of his

religion, 'It is doing me good', or something of the sort; but he need not: and it does not strike me that 'I am a Christian, but being one makes me thoroughly miserable, gives me no satisfaction, does me no good' is self-contradictory. Admittedly, one might so understand 'gives me no satisfaction', 'does me no good', in such a way that it would be self-contradictory; but then it becomes simply a matter of definition that religion gives one satisfaction, does one good. I take it that 'Being a Christian gives satisfaction, does one good', is intended to be synthetic, not analytic; and I should say, taking those phrases at what seems to be their face-value, that it is as likely to be false as true. Religion may help to provide integration for some, but may feed the neuroses of others.

Further, there are those who are content to say: All religions are equal, without adding: But some are more equal than others. The addition, as far as I can see, does need to be made by the Christian, and Jung is not of much help to those who think it is important to make it. Neither is Freud, if it comes to that; but then Freud is not writing as a supporter, even an ambiguous supporter, of religion.

Discussions of the relation between psychology and religion tend to deal mainly with the implications of psycho-analysis and of Jung's analytical psychology; but the relevance to the theme of this book of more tough-minded approaches is also considerable. Dr. William Sargant's *Battle for the Mind* brings together conveniently a number of things that are missed by the approach that limits itself to Freud and Jung.

Dr. Sargant considers that the reason why preachers are not particularly successful in converting the masses today is that they tend to appeal too much to the intellect. It is not rational argumentation that converts, but emotional appeal. So far this is just the expression of a conventional view of a certain kind. Dr. Sargant seeks to justify it and to build upon it by making use of some of Pavlov's experimental findings, and the findings of psychologists who were concerned with wartime neuroses. He stresses the importance of basic temperamental types for the effectiveness of conversion. On the whole, the person most open to conversion is the 'normal' conventional individual, the suggestible person most inclined to conform to whatever seems to be expected of him. The effective method of conversion is, roughly, this: the subject's emotions must be worked on 'until he reaches an abnormal condition of anger, fear or exaltation'. This condition is maintained or intensified and 'hysteria may supervene, whereupon the subject can become more open to suggestions which in normal circumstances he would have summarily rejected. Alternatively, the equivalent or the paradoxical and ultra-paradoxical phases may occur. [The equivalent phase is that in which "the brain gives the same response to both strong and weak stimuli"; the paradoxical that in which "the brain responds more actively to weak stimuli than to strong"; the ultra-paradoxical that in which "conditioned responses and behaviour patterns turn from positive to negative; or from negative to positive" (p. 14).] Or a sudden complete inhibitory collapse may bring about a suppression of previously held beliefs. All these happenings could be of help in bringing about new beliefs and behaviour patterns.' Methods of converting someone to new religious or political beliefs can be the same as those used in the treatment of neuroses and psychoses. 'All the different phases of brain activity, from an increased excitement to emotional exhaustion and collapse in a terminal stupor, can be induced either by psychological means; or by drugs; or by shock treatments, produced electrically; or by simply lowering the sugar content of the patient's blood with insulin injections. And some of the best results in the psychiatric treatment of neuroses and psychoses occur from the inducing of states of protective inhibition. This is often done by continuing artificially imposed stresses on the brain until a terminal stage of temporary emotional collapse and stupor is reached, after which, it seems that some of the new abnormal patterns may disperse, and the healthier one can return or be implanted afresh in the brain' (p. 16).

The techniques of religious conversion that Dr. Sargant discusses are psychological, presumably because no one has yet, as far as I know, attempted religious conversion by drugs, electric shocks or insulin injections. It is clear that he does not consider that there is any difference in principle between the psychological and the physiological techniques. Each is only a means to the same end, that of increasing or prolonging stress to the point of collapse where the subject is open to receiving a new set of beliefs and attitudes. (One religious sect whose activities are illustrated by photographs in the book sometimes call the final collapse phase 'wiping the slate clean' for God.) Dr. Sargant considers in detail the methods used by John Wesley and other successful evangelists. Chiefly, their preaching was designed to induce emotional collapse by dwelling on the pains of eternal damnation and only when collapse had occurred to offer the good news of salvation. He says: 'As Pavlov's experimental findings in dogs and experiences in the treatment of war neuroses would lead one to expect, the effect of getting too emotionally involved, either positively or negatively, with Wesley's preaching was to increase markedly the likelihood of being converted. It often happened, quite unexpectedly for the person concerned, that when he had been roused to the greatest pitch of indignation and anger by the proceedings, he suddenly broke down and accepted every belief demanded of him. For . . . anger, as well as fear, can induce disturbances of brain function which make a person highly suggestible and reverse his conditioned behaviour patterns, or even wipe the "cortical slate" clean' (p. 81).

The effect of Dr. Sargant's book, and of the work by himself and others which he expounds in it, is to suggest a version of the view that religion is non-rational. The book does not bear upon the question whether there are in fact good objective grounds for religious beliefs; but it suggests the view of an individual's religion—where this means certain of his beliefs, attitudes and practices—as something fairly readily inducible, in many people anyway, by what might naturally be called 'non-rational' methods. Religion, then, can be said to be non-rational in the sense of being inducible by certain 'mechanical' techniques or by psychological techniques which can essentially be classed with these. Techniques of 'persuasion' have been a good deal discussed in recent years, and 'rational' methods of persuasion distinguished from 'non-rational'. Where such a line should be drawn across the concept of persuasion, if at all, does not concern us; but it needs to be noted that *any* method of 'persuasion' might naturally be said to be 'rational' by contrast with such methods of inducing beliefs as drugs or shock-treatment; and the preaching of hell-fire might, reasonably enough, be called 'persuasion'. One chief interest of Dr. Sargant's *Battle for the Mind* is that it uses a classification of methods of inducing beliefs different from that which people might generally be inclined to make. A sermon by John Wesley, he might say, is more like a beating-up than it is like a sermon by Bishop Butler.

Another line that Dr. Sargant's book seems to draw in a place different from its usual place is that between 'genuine' and 'non-genuine' religious conversion. He does wish to make such a distinction, as, for instance, when he writes of 'genuine' religious conversions being seen after leucotomy operations (p. 70). (The sentence immediately following does not throw much light on the distinction: 'For the mind is freed from its old strait-jacket and new religious beliefs and attitudes can now more easily take the place of the old.') But he does not give his criteria for distinguishing a genuine conversion from a non-genuine one. A religious conversion induced by leucotomy—or by drugs, electric convulsive treatment, or insulin coma treatment—is just what we might be inclined to call *not* genuine. The criteria for 'genuine' and 'non-genuine' in religion are notoriously not settled; as we have already had occasion to note in connexion with religious experience (in Chapter 8). I do not wish to lay much stress on this point; for, as I have already remarked, no one has in fact yet induced religious conversions by physiological methods (I am excepting the techniques of the yogi or the Christian ascetic), so there has been no occasion to decide how 'genuine' and 'non-genuine' stand in the light of them; and certainly we do not deny the epithet 'genuine' to conversions induced by hell-fire preaching, which by Dr. Sargant's classification is the same kind of thing.

Dr. Sargant, as I have already said, considers that the reason why preachers today tend not to make a strong appeal to the masses is that their preaching is too much directed at their hearers' intellects and too little at their emotions. It is undoubtedly true that mild, intellectual preaching does not bring about religious revivals. Dr. Sargant wants to go further. He seems at times to equate *being religious* with being converted by revivalistic preaching. It is true that he writes in his Foreword: 'It must not be held against me that I do not discuss some types of purely intellectual conversion, but only those physical or psychological stimuli, rather than intellectual arguments, which seem to help to produce conversion by causing alterations in the subject's brain function. Hence the term "physiology" in the title.' (The book's subtitle is: 'A Physiology of Conversion and Brain-washing'. Actually it is something of a misnomer. The greater part of the discussion is of psychological, not physiological, techniques.) Certainly, he is not concerned with all kinds of conversion. The general slant of the book is nevertheless such as to suggest that the author on the whole thinks more highly of conversions induced by psychological or physiological pressure—that is, 'emotionally'—than of those brought about by argument. He writes, towards the end of the book (p. 234): 'Must a new concentration on brain physiology and brain mechanics weaken religious faith and beliefs? On the contrary, a better understanding of the means of creating and consolidating faith will enable religious bodies to expand much more rapidly. The preacher can rest assured that the less mysteriously "God works his wonders to perform", the easier it should be to provide people with an essential knowledge and love of God'.

Certainly, by the use of the methods Dr. Sargant discusses, religious bodies will expand more rapidly; but some religious people might consider preferable a state in which they expanded rather slowly but by other means. Fewer people respond to intellectual appeal than to emotional appeal—or than would to physiological methods if these were widely used. But how important are mere numbers? The methods of Wesley or Jonathan Edwards were more effective than those of their less 'enthusiastic' brethren, but the preacher may legitimately hesitate before embracing the methods of Wesley or Edwards when he sees that Dr. Sargant connects them with those of Hitler and Stalin. Effectiveness is surely not enough. Dr. Sargant does not explicitly raise the question: What is religion? There is perhaps an implied answer to it in his exclusive stress on *efficiency* in techniques of conversion; and it is not an answer that all other

N

Christians would accept. Would a religion so induced be worth having? Would it be religion? Dr. Sargant would answer Yes to both these questions. Some other Christians might answer Yes (reluctantly) to the second, but No to the first. Others might answer No to both. Dr. Sargant writes (p. 235): 'If this book has offended the religious or ethical susceptibilities of any reader, despite my efforts to avoid doing so, let me plead in extenuation the need of a greater understanding, by as many intelligent readers as possible, of the power and comparative simplicity of some of the methods here discussed. If we are to *promote true religion* [my italics], preserve our democratic ways of life and our hard-won civil liberties, we must learn to recognize that these same methods are being used for trivial or evil purposes instead of noble ones.' Dr. Sargant's use of 'true religion' here is odd.

Writing about some passages that he has quoted from Arthur Koestler, Dr. Sargant says; 'These clinical observations become still more interesting when he gives in non-religious terms the same sort of mystical experience that floods the literature of religious conversion. The fact is that mystical experiences, like sudden conversions, do not always arise from purely religious influences and stresses; they can sometimes be induced by chemical means—such as, for instance, mescaline, ether, and laughing gas' (p. 87). 'Belief in divine possession is very common at such times [of physical and emotional collapse], and so is the mystical trance—essentially similar to that experienced by so many Christian and other saints in cramped cells or under martyrdom, and vouchsafed to Koestler when threatened with shooting by the Franco forces' (p. 89). The equation of the experiences of Christian mystics with those that can be induced by taking mescalin or by other 'mechanical', or physiological, means, is an essential part of Dr. Sargant's position. But it does not make for clarity to run together all the kinds of experience that have been given the name 'mystical'. That experiences inducible by mescalin, etc., are of the same sort as, or essentially similar to, the experiences of mystics, needs argument, and Dr. Sargant supplies none.

His central thesis is: religious conversion can be achieved by a conditioning process. This thesis is fairly sharply opposed to

Freud's: that religion springs from the Super-ego. Conditioning-talk is different from Super-ego-talk; but whether or not these two kinds of talk are totally irreconcilable I do not know, or, at the moment, care. My interest in these theses is in so far as they bear upon the view of religion as non-rational. Nothing is *proved* about religion by Freud, Jung, or Sargant. They are best thought of as inviting us to look at religion from certain points of view.

In the next, and final, chapter we shall consider some aspects of religious language. This will make a fitting climax to the book; for the overriding interest of the contemporary philosopher, when he has turned to consider religion, has undoubtedly been in the nature of religious discourse. It is here, as we shall see, that there arises a peculiarly modern and an extremely acute version of the view that religion is irrational.

CHAPTER 12

Assertion and Analogy

IT MIGHT be claimed that religion is irrational in the sense that religious belief is not expressible in a set of meaningful assertions. The whole problem of the status of the putative assertions of religion has been a rather familiar inquiry among philosophers since the publication of Professor John Wisdom's 'Gods'. Before I come to tackle the question whether there are genuine assertions in religion I want to indicate the terminological apparatus that I shall use.

I want to make use (drawing here upon Jung—see Jung (1), pp. 601–2) of a distinction between 'literal' meaning, 'semiotic' meaning, and 'symbolical' meaning. The literal meaning of an utterance is its 'ordinary', its 'surface' meaning. 'Three white leopards sat under a juniper-tree' literally means neither more nor less than that three white leopards sat under a juniper-tree. Perhaps in a poem 'Three white leopards sat under a juniper-tree' might also have symbolical meaning. Where criticism is too revealing and provides reasonably adequate 'translations' of obscure poetic passages, saying what they mean in 'plain English', then those passages do *not* have symbolical meaning. An utterance with symbolical meaning, as this expression will be used in the present chapter, is one that cannot be 'explained' without its point being lost. (I do not suggest that this is what the expression means in ordinary speech; nor that this is necessarily what the expression meant in the previous chapter.) If the meaning of an utterance is not its 'ordinary', 'surface' meaning, but if it can nevertheless be explained without losing its point, then its meaning is not symbolical meaning but another kind of meaning, semiotic meaning.

My use of 'symbolical' may be thought to need some defence. A symbol is something that stands for something else, and one expects it to be possible to say *what* a given symbol stands for; but the point about 'symbolical meaning', as I have chosen to use the expression here, is that you cannot say what it is symbolical of. Why, then, call it symbolical? Because by contrast with 'literal meaning' the expression 'symbolical meaning' suggests distance from the object, obscurity; and it is these overtones that I have in mind in using the expression as I do. When we have a straightforward case of standing-for-something-else I use 'semiotic'. I do not say that utterances with symbolical meaning in my sense do not 'stand for' anything—for this would indeed make it pointless to use the term 'symbolical'—but rather that while sure they stand for something, we are sure also that we cannot explain in other words what it is that they do stand for.

This distinction is rough. It recognizes no difference between metaphors and codes. The notion of 'ordinary, surface meaning' needs tightening up; for the ordinary surface meaning of a metaphorical utterance could be said to be its meaning as a metaphor rather than what that set of words on a literal, non-metaphorical interpretation would mean. So does the notion of 'standing for' need clarification. Again, the dividing line between semiotic meaning and symbolical meaning is liable to vanish if looked at too closely: the distinction may arise simply from differences in our familiarity with the subject-matter, so that the line would not always be in the same place. In spite of all this, I hope the distinction is clear enough. In any case, what I am interested in is seeing what can be done if it is assumed as a starting point.

I am writing about three different kinds of meaning. The phrase 'different kinds of meaning' is, however, a misleading one; and I want to make plain what I intend by it. This might, I think, almost as well be expressed by saying that I am writing about different kinds of utterance—in the sense that a literal utterance is a different kind of utterance from a metaphorical utterance (or an empirical proposition from an *a priori* one, etc.);

this I choose to express by saying that one has literal meaning and the other semiotic meaning. To say that they have different kinds of meaning indicates that the meaning is in one case 'on the surface', and that the utterance is in need of no explanation, and in the other that it is being expressed by words used in an odd context, or in strained senses, and thus that the utterance is capable of explanation—though in practice probably not needing it. The point is that I do not mean something different by 'meaning' in each of the expressions 'literal meaning', 'semiotic meaning', and 'symbolical meaning': what difference in kind of meaning there is between utterances of the three types lies not in their 'quality of meaningfulness' but in what I can only call the methods by which their meaning is expressed. (Sometimes, I think, 'meaning' *is* qualified with the intention of indicating a different quality of meaningfulness. Compare the parallel case of 'true'. People say 'psychologically true', 'dramatically true', etc. Suppose someone asks, 'Is it true that Christ fed the five thousand?' To reply, 'Well, it's spiritually (or, etc.) true', may well strike the questioner as no more than a confusing way of saying that it is *not* true. The multiplication of different kinds of meaning and truth, in *this* sense, provides too easy an 'answer' to difficulties about the meaningfulness or truth of religious utterances.)

In religion there are utterances of all these kinds. (*a*) 'Jesus was born in Bethlehem' would, on the whole, be said to have literal meaning. (*b*) 'God is our Father' has semiotic meaning. It is a metaphor; or, it states or implies an analogy; or, it is an *as-if* statement; or, it uses a familiar relation to stand for a much more difficult one that could only be otherwise expressed at length. (*c*) 'God is One Person in Three Persons', and 'God was incarnate in Jesus Christ', perhaps have symbolical meaning; these, one might say, cannot be explained in simple, literal terms—or perhaps in any terms—and attempts so to explain them result only in their real point vanishing. (The Athanasian Creed, for instance, is not an explanation of the doctrine of the Trinity but an extended statement of it.) They are Christian 'mysteries'.

These three kinds of meaning are not mutually exclusive; I have suggested this already: the same utterance on one occasion could be meant literally, on another semiotically or symbolically. Also, this classification is not meant to be exhaustive. We need to note, further, that there might be, and indeed are, differences of opinion among religious believers about the status of a given utterance: clearly, there is not the same agreement among Christians about the status of, say, 'Christ walked on the water', or 'He shall come to judge the quick and the dead', as there is about that of, say, 'Jesus was born in Bethlehem'.

So much for the apparatus. Now for the question.

Any view which says that religious people, when they talk about God, do not intend to make assertions, would undoubtedly be rejected by the ordinary believer. If he has occasion to talk about God he undoubtedly means to make assertions; he is not likely to say, unprompted, that he is expressing his feelings, or uttering sounds because he thinks them pleasant. A missionary, in his attempts to convert the heathen, will spend a fair amount of his time in trying to impart information. There is one God, he will say, if that needs to be said; and Jesus Christ is the Son of God. The Son of God lived on earth in human form for a period of years, and during those years, among other things, he taught. And these are some of his teachings. . . . God is our Father and we are his children. God loves us and watches over us. God wants us to love him and also our fellow men. . . . More important than his teachings was himself, and what he did for us in his death, which took place in a particularly horrible way, and was followed by a miraculous resurrection. . . . What precisely the missionary will say will depend on the missionary himself and on the Christian body that is responsible for him. Much of what he says will consist in assertions, or putative assertions. There is no doubt that he *intends* many of his utterances as assertions. But the question is: are they?

What has become the standard argument on this is Professor Antony Flew's (see Flew and MacIntyre, pp. 96–9). Professor Flew's point is this: To assert is always also to deny. The person who asserts *p* must intend to deny *not-p*, and if he is not denying anything then he is not asserting anything either. Now the religious believer, who says 'God exists', or 'God has a plan',

or 'God loves us as a father loves his children', seems unwilling
to admit evidence as telling against his belief. The belief that God
is love, for instance, does not seem to be affected by evidence of
any amount or any kind of suffering. All that happens is that the
original assertion is qualified and qualified (God's love is 'not a
merely human love'; or it is 'an inscrutable love' . . .) until, as
Professor Flew puts it, it 'dies the death of a thousand qualifications'.

Let us call this argument 'the falsification argument'; viz., the
putative assertions of the religious believer are not really assertions because they are incapable of falsification. The argument is
directed, I take it, against utterances with semiotic or symbolical
meaning, and can be crudely represented as a complaint that
these are not meant literally.

This argument is not as straightforward as it looks. If we are
in doubt as to whether someone is really asserting something,
says Professor Flew, 'one way of trying to understand (or perhaps
it will be to expose) his utterance is to attempt to find what he
would regard as counting against, or as being incompatible with,
its truth' (p. 98). It is not altogether clear what this means.
'Trying to understand (or perhaps it will be to expose)' an utterance looks like trying to find out what it *means*, or whether it
means anything; attempting to find out what the utterer would
regard as counting against its truth looks more like (a roundabout
way of) trying to find out what makes him say it, or, on what
grounds he wants to *assert* it as true. There seems to be a confusion
here. Of course, an utterance must be meaningful if it is to be
judged either true or false; but it does not follow from our being
unable to judge it either true or false that it is meaning*less*.

There is an ambiguity in the notion of an utterance not being
a real assertion as Professor Flew uses it. It is not clear whether
his objection to religious putative assertions is that what they say
cannot be either verified or falsified, or that they are meaningless,
that is, they do not really say anything. He seems to want to make
both these objections, the second, illegitimately, on the basis of
the first. But these two things ought to be kept distinct. We need
to ask: Are religious putative assertions meaningful and, Are they
really assertions (i.e. are they true-or-false)? However, let us

leave this for the moment and consider the falsification argument as it stands.

There are two natural counters to the falsification argument. To the suggestion that the apparent assertions of the religious believer are not really assertions at all the believer may find it natural to reply either: (*a*) Yes, they are, but they are assertions of a special kind which escape the falsification argument; or (*b*) They are not meant to be assertions, anyway, but something else. Neither of these counters will do—not, anyway, without considerable refinement.

(*a*) Assertions are assertions. What can be called different kinds of assertion do not differ from each other in the respect that they are assertions but in respect of some other, attached, properties. This I have already indicated. Thus, one can say that metaphorical (semiotic) assertions are a different kind of assertion from straightforward (literal) assertions: but the difference does not lie in their having different qualities of assertiveness; the difference is the difference between being a metaphor and not being a metaphor. Whatever 'kind' religious putative assertions be said to belong to, in so far as they are alleged to be assertions the falsification argument stands. So long as religious assertions are considered to have semiotic meaning they seem to be in danger of dying the death of a thousand qualifications. They do perhaps escape the danger if they are interpreted as having only symbolical meaning: but to regard *all* religious assertions as having only symbolical meaning will not do; it is perverse to regard 'God loves us' or 'God is our Father' as anything other than an analogical statement—that is, it is natural to class it as having semiotic meaning. (Actually, symbolical utterances, though meaningful, may well not be *assertions*; see later in the present chapter.)

(*b*) The second counter takes, crudely, the form of 'the attitude view': The man who talks about God—says that he exists and that he loves his creatures—is not asserting something so much as 'worshipping', or 'expressing his attitude to the universe' (two very different things, incidentally), or something else of the sort. This view is hardly satisfactory. Certainly, the religious man has an attitude, or one of several attitudes; but there is more to religion than that. It is implausible to suggest that, in effect, 'God exists' or 'God loves us', has only an emotive and not a descriptive use. (Worshipping is not best characterized as 'emotive'; but I am not here attempting to distinguish among the views that can conveniently be put together under the heading 'the attitude view'.) Any counter to the falsification argument that depends on such division of linguistic function will not do. I shall not discuss the attitude view in any detail in the remainder of the chapter.

The interest of the falsification argument lies in the problem it creates for those who wish to maintain the rational character of religion. The Thomist, for example, seems bound to say that the assertions of religion are genuine assertions—though perhaps not 'ordinary' assertions but 'assertions of a special kind'. The impressive structure of the Thomist Doctrine of Analogy is intended to explain, on the assumption that talk about God is meaningful assertion, just what sort of assertions assertions about God are. But, according to the falsification argument, what appear to be assertions in religion may not be meaningful assertions at all.

I want to say more about the first of the natural counters to the falsification argument—the reply, that is, that religious assertions are assertions, but assertions which escape the argument through being assertions of a special kind. I shall consider this line of escape in so far as it takes one, or both, of the forms: (1) the assertions of religion have not literal but semiotic meaning, or (2) they have not literal but symbolical meaning.

I shall limit myself mainly to utterances about God. It is arguable that all religious utterances are 'in the end' about God; but certainly only some are so explicitly, and these need to be marked off from the others.

The view of religious utterances as having semiotic meaning is widely held. Indeed, the view that in general when we talk about God we talk metaphorically or analogically is, I suppose, that most usually subscribed to. Men, because the most important things that they want to say about God can only be said by means of metaphors, analogies, parables, are in danger of failing to say anything at all. For, to put it bluntly, they never mean just what they say; and when pressed to say what they do mean they tend to utter more metaphors, and when they are pressed for the meaning of *those* they may, as Professor Flew suggests, qualify, and qualify, and qualify. . . .

Now the Christian wants to say of his analogies and metaphors that they are 'true'. On what grounds does he say this?

As a matter of fact, we do not use 'true' and 'false' of analogies and metaphors as frequently as we use, say, 'apt' or 'good', or 'bad'. (For instance, on the occasions when we say 'How true!' of a metaphorical or analogical statement we more often than not might equally as well have said, 'What a good way of putting it!' This is certainly not what we usually intend when we say 'How true!' of a statement meant literally: 'This film is going on just a bit too long.'—'How true!') This, of course, is far from settling any difficulties about what is meant by calling a semiotic statement true, but it at least indicates that some light may be thrown on this by following up 'apt' or 'good' in these contexts rather than 'true'.

'Good' analogies are those that make their point simply and clearly; and they are those that are fruitful—those that suggest naturally the possibility of development in more than one direction, those that help to bring out connexions that we might have overlooked. In religion, the analogies that strike people as the best are those used by Jesus, or biblical analogies generally. (Of course, these may also strike us as the best because they are the *authorized* analogies.) There is simplicity, fruitfulness, 'timelessness', about the analogy of Fatherhood used of God. Some of the biblical analogies, like that of Shepherd, may mean less to us than to people in other times or places, but they are still simple, 'elemental'.

It seems hardly relevant to ask: Is it *true* that God's relation to us is that of the father in the parable of the Prodigal Son to (chiefly) his younger son? It seems even less relevant to ask: Is God *really* a shepherd? The point is that analogies are often tendered in explanation of things that cannot be expressed in any but analogical, metaphorical, indirect, ways. We are not reduced to analogy when we want to say that a film has gone on too long, but we are when we want to talk about God. There is often no alternative statement—no simple, non-analogical, literal, statement—that will do the job we want done. If there were such a statement available we should not have been reduced in the first place to using analogies and metaphors in order to say what we wanted to say. Sometimes we choose to talk metaphorically for literary or similar reasons, but most talk about God is essentially metaphorical or analogical.

A view which may suggest itself is that the utterances of religion are all semiotic and can only be explained in terms of each other. Perhaps they constitute a kind of semiotic system. To put this in more practical terms: it is as if the religious believer had confined himself within a circle of meaning. If a man stands outside the circle, waiting for some one religious belief to become clear to him before he will commit himself to a religious way of life, he will wait for ever. No religious belief, it might be said, can be explained in terms of other religious beliefs. The circle is closed. Once it is entered—by Kierkegaard's 'leap of faith', perhaps—the system, though not necessarily immediately or in all its parts, becomes plain. One analogy, metaphor, or parable throws light on another, and that on another, and so on. But it is not possible to take any one of them out of the system and explain it in terms other than those proper to the system.

There is a difficulty in this view. If we are to be able to say that statements are analogical, metaphorical, or parabolic, some at least of their terms must in the literal sense be understood by us. You can only know that 'The lion is the king of the beasts' is a metaphor if you know something, though it need not be much, about lions, or beasts, or kingship. You need, in fact, to know only enough to be able to see that the statement is not literal; that is, you need merely to know that kingship is literally a relationship that holds between human beings and it then follows that 'X is the king of the *beasts*' must be a metaphor (or false!). You need to know more than this, of course, to know that it is a good metaphor.

So, we may say, you can only know that 'God is our Father' is an analogy if you understand certain things about God or fatherhood—that is, certain non-analogical things. On the view that God is incomprehensible to human minds, it would be fatherhood that we should need to know something about rather than God; again, simply that it is literally a relation between human beings would be enough. Then, granted that 'God' is not the name of a human being, it follows that 'God is our Father' must be a metaphor. We can, in general, only see that a statement about A is a metaphorical or analogical statement if we are able to look at it alongside other statements about A that are *not* metaphorical or analogical statements. (In the case of God, negative statements—denying certain empirical qualities to him —would fit the bill.) Accordingly, it does not make sense to say that *all* religious statements have semiotic meaning; it would be pointless to say of some that they had semiotic meaning unless we were also prepared to say of others that they had literal meaning.

A similar point can be made about the *truth* of religious assertions, as we have already seen in the previous chapter. As I there pointed out, there is merit in the literal-minded approach to religious belief seen in a writer like Freud (especially when contrasted with Jung): religion must be either true or false, and in no fancy senses of 'true' and 'false' either. This kind of view does at least help to make plain that something in religion must be literally true if anything in it is to be 'semiotically true' (if I may use this expression). This, we may note, brings out the importance of the claim that Christianity is an 'historical religion'; for the characterization of it as 'historical' reminds us that propositions like 'Jesus was born in Bethlehem' are part of it as well as propositions like 'God is our Father'. Christianity is not simply a kind of timeless mythology. But the inclination to treat it thus is a strong one; for it is clear that what really matters in Christianity is not its rock-bottom historical basis but the superstructure erected upon it. The statement 'Jesus was born in Bethlehem' does not say anything that would be judged a really important religious belief: only if it is taken to mean 'The Son of God was born in Bethlehem' does it do this; and this latter statement, though certainly it can be called an historical statement, is an interpretation of what we may call the bare historical facts and not a simple statement of them. When we come to other important items of religious belief—like the Trinity—we are even further away from what is historical in any simple sense. The inclination to discount the historical element in Christianity is, then, strong. But to be reminded that Christianity is an historical religion is at least to be reminded that the more important of the expressions of Christian belief are anchored to some straightforward literal statements of the kind that historians must begin from. I shall say more about this anchoring at the end of the chapter.

I have been writing about religious assertions regarded as statements with semiotic meaning. Suppose someone is prepared to maintain the position that all, or at least all the really important, religious beliefs have purely symbolical meaning—a meaning inexplicable and irreducible. The view of religious utterances as having merely symbolical meaning may seem hardly distinguishable from the view of them as having no meaning—in the sense that the believer will be no more able to say to himself what his symbols mean than he is able to say this to anyone else. He *has* the symbols and they *do something for* him and he *feels* he understands something in and through them. The use of the term 'meaning' may well seem objectionable. I should agree that 'meaning' is being used here not in its commonest way. Yet it is sometimes used in this way. For instance, a man is not altogether talking nonsense who says: 'I now understand the meaning of human existence, but I cannot possibly explain it.'

Let us look more closely at the notion of symbolical meaning. It will help us if we follow up a fairly familiar parallel.

A parallel has quite frequently been drawn between the religious man and the artist, and we have already had occasion (in Chapter 2) to discuss this. At the risk of repetition, let us return to this theme. It has sometimes been said that the religious man, like the artist, is a person who has a kind of special insight into the nature of things; only that where one sees beauty the other sees God. As a description of 'the' artist this will hardly do; but it is perhaps a useful way of thinking of at least some of the people who are called artists. And it seems reasonable to say that there may be some insights that cannot be expressed in words, but only in music, painting, and so on; or, if in words, not in matter-of-fact literal statements, but in indirect, roundabout ways—in 'poetic language'. The well-known 'untranslatability' of art forms (referred to in Chapter 2) is significant here. You cannot 'translate' a piece of music into a poem, or a poem adequately into prose. You can come near to it, but you will not completely hit it off. Such 'translations' miss the point of the original work of art.

There are insights, then, that are conveyed best without words, and insights that are conveyed best when words are used in some ways and not in others. It seems natural to say that the non-verbal symbols of religion (e.g. the placing of lighted candles on an altar) are like the symbols of the non-literary artist. They perhaps express some things that words cannot express as well—and perhaps some of them express things that words cannot express at all. And the verbal symbols of religion are reminiscent of the uses of language by some literary artists. This links with the attitude view of religion. The attitude to the world of the religious man is the attitude appropriate towards something that is both concealing and revealing something else—something else that he thinks of great importance. In this he is like the artist; but the difference between them in this respect lies in the fact that although they both have attitudes they do not have the same attitude; though this is not to deny that some artists are religious men as well, and that their art is suffused with their religious attitude to the world.

Creative art combines expression and communication. The artist perhaps is saying: I have found something that I cannot tell you about in words—and yet that I cannot keep silent about; I want you to find it, too. Though admittedly not all artists have strongly the desire to 'communicate' with the world at large. Something like this can also be said of at least some religious men. Artists are people who create works of art; and what this obvious truth implies is that the artist is not someone who simply goes through mysterious inner experiences which may never show themselves outwardly. An artist is not usefully thought of as someone who first has an inner experience and then expresses it. His having an experience and his expressing it are better thought of as one. You cannot be a great painter and yet never have painted anything; a great writer and never have written anything. In this sense, art is expression. This artistic creation or expression is generally said to be by means of 'symbols', and although no doubt a symbol must be symbolic *of* something (or there would be no point in calling it a symbol), this does not mean that it must be possible to express what it is symbolic of in any other way (in particular, in any non-symbolic way).

Being an item in religious worship, whether a linguistic or a non-linguistic item, can itself be a heading in the classification of kinds of human behaviour. The view that finds symbolic meaning in religious utterances is perhaps saying something like this: What the linguistic and non-linguistic symbols of religion have in common is more important than what they differ in. Neither, say, the Athanasian Creed, when recited in a context of worship, nor the cross on a church's altar, asserts anything about God in a way that lends itself to simple or complete explanation. There will always be mystery. It would sound strange, in fact, to say of the cross that it *asserted* anything. The view we are considering invites us to agree that the fact that a recitation of the Athanasian Creed involves the uttering of sentences in the indicative mood does not imply that in reciting it we are asserting anything either. Symbolic religious utterances are meaningful but are not assertions.

I should not, of course, want to recommend the view that *all* religious utterances have merely symbolical meaning. Some religious utterances are clearly best thought of as semiotic, and others as literal. But some religious utterances can usefully be thought of as having symbolical meaning: and this helps to preserve the element of mystery which, it seems, is essential to religion.

Let us return to our question. Is religious belief expressible in a set of meaningful assertions? This question, as we noted, has two halves—are expressions of religious belief meaningful, and are they assertions?

There are among religious beliefs some intended to have literal meaning. These certainly are meaningful. They are also certainly assertions; the Christian cannot dispute that the belief, say, that Jesus of Nazareth was born in Bethlehem in 4 B.C. is one that could be supported or refuted by evidence.

Utterances with literal meaning are not of central importance for religion; and, in any case, as I said above, the falsification argument is directed not against them but against what I am calling utterances with semiotic and symbolic meaning. What are we to say about these?

I may seem already to have begged one half of the question by writing of semiotic 'meaning' and symbolical 'meaning'. If I now simply repeat that semiotic and symbolical utterances are meaningful this may seem like altogether too short a way with the dissenters. Yet this is the right thing to say. We show what a semiotic utterance means by explaining the metaphor or analogy. 'God is our Father' means 'God's relation to us is in respects *a*, *b*, *c*, like that of a father to his children'; just as 'The lion is the king of the beasts' means 'The lion's relation to other beasts is in respects *a*, *b*, *c*, like that of a king to his subjects.' The case of symbolical utterances is less clear. We might say that 'God is One Person in Three Persons' means what, for instance, the Athanasian Creed says it means, but this does not really help; for, as I suggested earlier, the Athanasian Creed is not really an explanation but an extended statement of the Doctrine of the Trinity. I prefer to say, rather, that 'God is One Person in Three Persons' is meaningful but not explicable. This, as I have said earlier, is not a common sense of 'meaningful'; but I have also already mentioned my motive in wanting to use it in this way— my desire to preserve a place in this account of religious discourse for the element of mystery.

Are semiotic and symbolical religious utterances assertions? In the case of symbolical utterances, probably not. In the case of semiotic utterances, yes—in the sense that they are anchored to assertions with literal meaning. This anchoring is what makes them true-or-false (and hence assertions). What precisely is to be understood here by the metaphor of anchoring?

We have three things to consider in the case of a semiotic utterance.

(1) The utterance itself. 'God is our Father', say, or, 'God loves us as a father loves his children'.

(2) Its meaning. 'God is our Father' means 'God's relation to us is in respects $a, b, c, \ldots$ like that of a father to his children'. ($a, b, c, \ldots$ might be cashed as follows: all men are brothers; God will punish the wicked and reward the virtuous; God watches with deep interest and concern all our doings. . . . The metaphors here themselves call for further explanation, of course.)

(3) Its anchoring. To give the anchor of 'God is our Father' is to state the reasons that make us want to assert it. Or, if you like, to say how it is anchored is to answer the question: What makes you say that? It is a defect of the falsification argument that it does not distinguish meaning from anchoring; that is, it does not distinguish meaning from truth. The anchor may take, for example, the following form: 'I completely recovered from my serious illness last year, after prayer'. Now this, of course, does not mention God, and there is no logical step from 'I completely recovered from my serious illness last year, after prayer' to 'God is our Father'. Nevertheless, 'I completely recovered from my serious illness last year, after prayer' is, I think, the kind of thing a man might say in giving his reasons for wanting to assert 'God is our Father'. Recoveries from illness, after prayer, constitute grounds for asserting 'God is our Father'; as 'undeserved' suffering constitutes grounds for denying it. In other words, *evidence* is relevant as tending to confirm or disconfirm semiotic religious assertions (though not relevant to symbolical religious utterances—which is why they are not assertions).

Bibliography

The Bibliography is intended both to provide details of works quoted from or mentioned in the course of this book and to offer suggestions for further reading in the Philosophy of Religion.

ABBOTT, T. K. See Kant (2).

ANSELM. *Proslogion.* Translations of the complete text may be found in A. C. Pegis, *The Wisdom of Catholicism* (Random House: New York, 1949); or in E. R. Fairweather (editor and translator) *A Scholastic Miscellany: Anselm to Ockham* (Vol. X of The Library of Christian Classics. S.C.M. Press: London, 1956); or in S. N. Dean, *St. Anselm: Proslogium; Monologium; an Appendix on Behalf of the Fool by Gaunilon; and Cur Deus Homo* (Open Court Publishing Co.: Chicago, 1930 (1903)). Translations of the chapters on the Ontological Argument only may also be found in Caldecott and Mackintosh or in Smart (3).

AQUINAS, THOMAS. *Summa Theologica*, literally translated by the fathers of the English Dominican Province (Vols. I–XXII) (Burns, Oates & Washbourne: London, 1920–28). See Vol. I. For the Five Ways see also Smart (3) or Caldecott and Mackintosh.

AUGUSTINE. *De Libero Arbitrio*, translated in *Augustine: Earlier Writings*, Vol. VI of The Library of Christian Classics (S.C.M. Press: London, 1953).

AYER, A. J. (1). *Language, Truth and Logic*, 2nd edn. (Gollancz: London, 1946).

AYER, A. J. (2). 'The Vienna Circle', in *The Revolution in Philosophy*, G. Ryle (editor) (Macmillan: London, 1956).

AYER, A. J. (3). (editor). *Logical Positivism* (Allen & Unwin: London, 1959).

AYER, A. J. and COPLESTON, F. C. 'Logical Positivism—a Debate', in *A Modern Introduction to Philosophy*: readings from classical and contemporary sources, editors Paul Edwards and Arthur Pap (Allen & Unwin: London, 1957).

BARTH, K. *Anselm: Fides Quaerens Intellectum*, Ian W. Robertson (translator) (S.C.M. Press: London, 1960).

BERKELEY, G. *Three Dialogues between Hylas and Philonous*, in Vol. 2 of Berkeley's *Works* in nine volumes, A. Luce and T. E. Jessop (editors) (Nelson: London and Edinburgh, 1948–57).

BRADLEY, F. H. *Appearance and Reality*. A Metaphysical Essay (Clarendon Press: Oxford, 1946 (1893)).

BRAITHWAITE, R. B. *An Empiricist's View of the Nature of Religious Belief* (Cambridge University Press: Cambridge, 1955).

BROAD, C. D. *Religion, Philosophy and Psychical Research* (Routledge & Kegan Paul: London, 1953).

BUTLER, J. *The Analogy of Religion, Natural and Revealed, to the Constitution and Course of Nature*, first published 1736 (Oxford University Press: Oxford, 1844). Various other editions available.

CALDECOTT, A. and MACKINTOSH, H. R. (editors and translators). *Selections from the Literature of Theism* (T. & T. Clark: Edinburgh, 3rd edn. 1931). This contains extracts from Anselm, Aquinas, Descartes, and Kant among others. The principles of inclusion and exclusion with which the editors operate reflect to some extent the attitudes of the time at which the book was originally published (1904). See also Smart (3).

The Cloud of Unknowing. There is a very readable version in modern English by Clifton Wolters in the Penguin Classics Series (Penguin: London, 1961).

COPLESTON, F. C. *Aquinas* (Penguin: London, 1955). See also Ayer and Copleston.

D'ARCY, M. C. *The Pain of this World and the Providence of God* (Longmans, Green: London, 1935).

DARWIN, C. *Origin of Species*, first published 1859. Various editions.

DESCARTES, R. *Meditations*, in Vol. I of *The Philosophical Works of Descartes*, Elizabeth S. Haldane and G. R. T. Ross (translators), in two vols. (Cambridge University Press: Cambridge, 1911). Various other editions.

DUCASSE, C. J. *A Critical Examination of the Belief in a Life after Death* (Charles C. Thomas: Springfield, Illinois, 1961).

EDWARDS, D. L. (editor). *The Honest to God Debate*. Some reactions to the book *Honest to God* (S.C.M. Press: London 1963). See also Robinson.

FARRER, A. *Finite and Infinite*: a philosophical essay (Dacre Press: London, 1943).

FERRÉ, F. *Language, Logic and God* (Eyre & Spottiswoode: London, 1962).

FLEW, A. and MACINTYRE, A. C. (editors). *New Essays in Philosophical Theology* (S.C.M. Press: London, 1955). A collection of essays by sixteen contemporary British philosophers applying modern philosophical techniques to some of the main problems in the Philosophy of Religion.

FREUD, S. (1). 'Obsessive Actions and Religious Practices' (1907), in Vol. IX of the Standard Edition of the *Complete Psychological Works of Sigmund Freud* (Hogarth Press: London, 1959).

FREUD, S. (2). *Totem and Taboo*, in Vol. XIII of the Standard Edition (Hogarth Press: London, 1955).

FREUD, S. (3). *On the History of the Psycho-analytic Movement*, in Vol. XIV of the Standard Edition (Hogarth Press: London, 1957).

FREUD, S. (4). *The Future of an Illusion*, W. D. Robson-Scott (translator) (Hogarth Press: London, 1949 (1928)).

FREUD, S. (5). *Moses and Monotheism*, Katherine Jones (translator) (Hogarth Press: London, 1939).

GAUNILO. See Anselm.

HEPBURN, R. W. (1). *Christianity and Paradox* (Watts: London, 1958).

HEPBURN, R. W. (2). 'From World to God', in *Mind*, January 1963 (Vol. LXXII, No. 285).

HICK, J. H. 'God as Necessary Being', in *The Journal of Philosophy*, October 27 and November 10, 1960 (Vol. LVII, Nos. 22 and 23).

HUME, D. *Dialogues concerning Natural Religion*, N. Kemp Smith (editor) 2nd edn. (Nelson: London and Edinburgh, 1947). The *Dialogues* are also included along with Hume's other writings on religion in *Hume on Religion*, editor R. Wollheim, in the Fontana Library (Collins: London, 1963).

HUXLEY, A. (1). *The Perennial Philosophy* (Chatto & Windus: London, 1946).

HUXLEY, A. (2). *The Doors of Perception* (Chatto & Windus: London, 1954).

HUXLEY, A. (3). *Heaven and Hell* (Chatto & Windus: London, 1956).

JAMES, W. *The Varieties of Religious Experience* (Longmans, Green: New York and London, 1902). Other editions.

JONES, E. *Sigmund Freud*, three vols. (Hogarth Press: London 1953–57).

JUNG, C. G. (1). *Psychological Types*, H. Godwin Baynes (translator) (Routledge & Kegan Paul: London, 1949 (1923)).

JUNG, C. G. (2). *Psychology and Religion*, Vol. 11 of the *Collected Works of C. G. Jung*, R. F. C. Hull (translator) (Routledge & Kegan Paul: London, 1958).

KANT, I. (1). *Critique of Pure Reason*, N. Kemp Smith (translator) (Macmillan: London, 1950 (1929)).

KANT, I. (2). *Critique of Practical Reason*, and other works on the theory of ethics, T. K. Abbott (translator) (Longmans, Green: London, 1948 (1909)).

KANT, I. (3). *Religion within the Boundary of Pure Reason*, J. W. Semple (translator) (Thomas Clark: Edinburgh, 1838). There is also a later (1934) translation by T. M. Greene and H. A. Hudson.

KIERKEGAARD, S. Most of Kierkegaard's writings are of interest to the philosopher of religion. See, e.g. *Concluding Unscientific Postscript*, D. F. Swenson and W. Lowrie (translators) (Princeton University Press: Princeton, N. J., 1944).

KNOWLES, D. *The English Mystical Tradition* (Burns & Oates: London, 1961).

LEWIS, C. S. *The Problem of Pain* (Bles: London, 1940).

LEWIS, H. D. *Our Experience of God* (Allen & Unwin: London, 1959).

MACINTYRE, A. C. See, Flew and MacIntyre.

MAIRET, P. (editor). *Christian Essays in Psychiatry* (S.C.M. Press: London, 1956).

MALCOLM, N. 'Anselm's Ontological Arguments', in *The Philosophical Review*, 1960 (Vol. LXIX); reprinted in N. Malcolm, *Knowledge and Certainty*. Essays and Lectures (Prentice Hall: Englewood Cliffs, N.J., 1963).

MARTIN, C. B. *Religious Belief* (Cornell University Press: Ithaca, New York, 1959).

MASCALL, E. L. (1). *Christ, the Christian and the Church* (Longmans, Green: London, 1946).

MASCALL, E. L. (2). *Existence and Analogy* (Longmans, Green: London, 1949).

McINTYRE, J. *St. Anselm and His Critics* (Oliver & Boyd: Edinburgh, 1954).

MITCHELL, B. (editor). *Faith and Logic* (Allen & Unwin: London, 1957). A collection of essays by Oxford philosophers who are also Anglicans.

MOWRER, O. H. *The Crisis in Psychiatry and Religion* (Van Nostrand: Princeton, N. J., 1961).

NEWMAN, J. H. *An Essay in Aid of a Grammar of Assent*. First published 1870, and reprinted in various editions, e.g. in Image Books (Doubleday: New York, 1955).

OTTO, R. *The Idea of the Holy*, J. W. Harvey (translator) (Oxford University Press: London, 1939 (1923)).

PALEY, W. *Works*. Various editions.

PARKINSON, C. N. *Parkinson's Law, or the Pursuit of Progress* (Murray: London, 1958).

RHINE, J. B. (1). *Extra-Sensory Perception* (Faber: London, 1935).

RHINE, J. B. (2). *New Frontiers of the Mind* (Faber: London, 1937).

RHINE, J. B. (3). *The Reach of the Mind* (Faber: London, 1948).

ROBINSON, J. A. T. *Honest to God* (S.C.M. Press: London, 1963). See also Edwards.

RYLE, G. *The Concept of Mind* (Hutchinson: London, 1949). See also Ayer (2).

SARGANT, W. *Battle for the Mind* (Heinemann: London, 1957).

SHAFFER, J. 'Existence, Predication, and the Ontological Argument', *Mind*, July 1962 (Vol. LXXI, No. 283).

SILLEM, E. A. *Ways of Thinking about God*: Thomas Aquinas and some recent problems (Darton, Longman & Todd: London, 1961).

SMART, N. (1). *Reasons and Faiths*: an investigation of religious discourse, Christian and non-Christian (Routledge & Kegan Paul: London, 1958).

SMART, N. (2). *A Dialogue of Religions* (S.C.M. Press: London, 1960).

SMART, N. (3). *Historical Selections in the Philosophy of Religion* (S.C.M. Press: London, 1962). Similar in plan to Caldecott and Mackintosh (q.v.), but reflecting better than that work what would nowadays be thought to be of most importance in past writings on the Philosophy of Religion.

SMART, N. (4). *Philosophers and Religious Truth* (S.C.M. Press: London, 1964).

TENNANT, F. R. *Philosophical Theology*, two vols. (Cambridge University Press: Cambridge, 1928, 1930).

VIDLER, A. R. and others. *Objections to Christian Belief* (Constable: London, 1963).

WEBB, C. C. J. *Kant's Philosophy of Religion* (Clarendon Press: Oxford, 1926).

WHITE, V. *God and the Unconscious* (Harvill Press: London, 1952).

WISDOM, J. 'Gods'. First published in *Proceedings of the Aristotelian Society*, 1944–45; reprinted in *Logic and Language*: First Series, A. G. N. Flew (editor) (Blackwell: Oxford, 1951), and in J. Wisdom, *Philosophy and Psycho-analysis* (Blackwell: Oxford, 1953).

WITTGENSTEIN, L. *Tractatus Logico-Philosophicus*, D. F. Pears and B. F. McGuinness (translators) (Routledge & Kegan Paul: London, 1961).

ZAEHNER, R. C. *Mysticism Sacred and Profane* (Clarendon Press: Oxford, 1957).

Index